ADVANCE PRAISE

"I hope every male financial advisor reads this book because it prepares them for what's about to come: a new period in finance where the different needs, approaches, and goals of women investors will change the face of investing itself."

—Joe Keefe, President and CEO,
Pax World Management

"*Harness the Power of the Purse* provides insightful guidance and a tactical roadmap for financial advisors and their managers offering a deeper understanding of how to meet the unique needs of women investors."

—Kathleen Lynch, COO,
UBS Wealth Management Americas

"Andrea Turner Moffitt's book provides data-driven support for a simple yet profound idea: aligning investments and values matters. This book will inspire individual investors who believe in market-based opportunities to create positive societal impact, while providing financial services professionals with an understanding as to why their clients, especially women, are seeking opportunities to invest in this way. And we will all be better off for it."

—Bruce Usher, Former CEO of EcoSecurities and
Director of the Tamer Center for Social Enterprise,
Columbia Business School

"*Harness the Power of the Purse* uncovers one of the most significant market growth opportunities for banks: women. I hope the financial industry pays close attention to the data and insights shared here so we can begin to see the game-changing impact women investors can have as economic powerhouses."

—Mary Ellen Iskenderian, President and CEO,
Women's World Banking

HARNESS

THE POWER

OF THE

PURSE

HARNESS
THE POWER
OF THE
PURSE

WINNING WOMEN INVESTORS

ANDREA TURNER MOFFITT

FOREWORD BY SYLVIA ANN HEWLETT

A VIREO BOOK | RARE BIRD BOOKS
LOS ANGELES, CALIF.

Moffitt, Andrea Turner.
    Harness the power of the purse : winning women investors /
Andrea Turner Moffitt ; foreword by Sylvia Ann Hewlett.
    p. cm.
    ISBN 978-1-940207-96-4
    Includes bibliographical references and index.

1. Women—Finance, Personal. 2. Finance, Personal. 3. Investments.
4. Women—Economic conditions. 5. Financial security. 6. Portfolio
management. 7. Wealth—Management. I. Hewlett, Sylvia Ann, 1946-.
II. Title.

HG4521 .M63 2015
332.0240082—dc23

For women investors around the world
May this inspire us to amplify our voice, leverage our
economic power, and be a catalyst for change

CONTENTS

FOREWORD

In 2013, the Center for Talent Innovation made an extraordinary step forward: we quantified the effect of diversity on bottom-lines.

We'd long understood, as had many global leaders in our Task Force, that a workforce diversified by gender, generation, geography, ethnicity, and sexual orientation was good for business. Leaders knew that having sales and marketing folks who "looked like the market" helped the firm connect to that market. We took this much further and posited that having people in R&D who represented target markets might similarly offer a competitive edge: who better to identify unmet needs and market opportunities among underserved populations than members of those populations? Research by social scientist Scott Page had affirmed the wisdom of crowds; Page showed mathematically that diversity trumps ability when it comes to solving thorny problems or predicting outcomes. If so, could we show that diverse teams were more innovative than homogeneous teams? And that diverse companies enjoyed, as a result of their innovation, greater market share?

Bringing our own diverse team to the endeavor, we embarked on a two-year research quest. We surveyed

1,800 college-educated professionals in the US, 700 of whom worked for multinational companies. We interviewed some 60 executives and innovators. We held focus groups with team leaders across industry sectors. And we generated 35 case studies of innovation that had derived from diverse teams. What we found, intriguingly, was that innovation depended on having two kinds of workforce diversity: *inherent* (inborn, immutable traits such as gender, ethnicity, and sexual orientation) and *acquired* (a sensitivity to difference gained through experience). Inherent diversity, as we had hypothesized, helped ensure that teams tasked with identifying unmet needs and innovating for them had the end-user insight they needed to succeed. Acquired diversity turned out to be highly correlated with inclusive leader behaviors, behaviors that unlocked the contribution of every team member and tapped everyone's toolkit to create the "speak-up culture" so critical to sustained problem-solving. We were able to show that companies with leadership manifesting both inherent and acquired diversity (what we termed "2D Diversity®") measurably outperformed companies that lacked it in terms of both innovation and market growth. Employees at these companies were 75% more likely than employees at non-diverse companies to say that their ideas were developed and implemented. They were 45% more likely to report that their firm's market share grew over the previous year and 70% more likely to report that the firm had captured a new market.

Our findings, which we published in a report entitled *Innovation, Diversity, and Market Growth,* caused a sensation. *Harvard Business Review* published our research, as did the *Stanford Social Innovation Review.* Our quest had culminated in the Holy Grail: a robust business case demonstrating that diversity unlocks innovation and growth.

Andrea Turner Moffitt was quick to perceive its implications in finance. As a former banker, a female professional, and a proactive investor, Andrea knew firsthand how poorly the industry connected with women, both in terms of its female talent and also with its female clientele. She was eager to apply our research to her field, to explore how inclusive leadership and our insights into acquired diversity could help advisors discover new ways to work with women, both as colleagues and as clients.

A wealth of industry data suggested that women comprised an enormous purse, with control of some $20 trillion of assets worldwide. Yet from Andrea's personal and professional work, it was apparent that most of that money lay on the table. Women weren't leveraging their wealth because wealth advisors ignored them or misunderstood their needs and wants.

As a research organization dedicated to helping women fulfill their leadership potential and to helping Fortune 500 companies better leverage female talent, CTI had its work cut out for itself: We would measure the disconnect globally. We would quantify the US purse (the amount of unleveraged wealth held by women). And on the strength of our findings from "Innovation, Diversity and Market Growth," we would map a way forward that would benefit both the industry and the women it employed and served.

Thus was born our Power of the Purse research stream. Under Andrea's leadership, we published *Harnessing the Power of the Purse: Female Investors and Global Opportunities for Growth*, the first in a series which has grown to encompass women in healthcare and is soon to study women in technology. It's a call to action but, more importantly, a blueprint for industry-wide change. We've provided advisors with a new toolkit of behaviors and tactics that will close the gap with the new market segments we identify. Andrea's familiarity with the industry and commitment to helping women take control of their wealth has infused this blueprint with invaluable energy and expertise. I am enormously pleased to have collaborated on this research and, with her, to share it.

—Sylvia Ann Hewlett, Founder and CEO,
Center for Talent Innovation

INTRODUCTION

My Story

On a warm summer afternoon in 2011, I joined a group of women working on Wall Street for lunch at a local café. After catching up on family and work, we plunged into a vibrant discussion of global challenges, kicking off with obstacles women face in finance. We bemoaned the stubbornly low numbers of female business leaders on the Street, and indeed across all industries. We debated why it was so difficult for our female entrepreneur friends to secure funding. Naturally, we landed on the perpetual discussion of the balancing act—career, family, and how to have it all.

But there was one topic we rarely touched on: money. Given our collective expertise as educated, opinionated women working in finance, I found this baffling. All day we discussed financing and investment strategies—just not our own and certainly not with each other. Privately, I had given a lot of thought to how we might invoke our capital and financial know-how to tackle our desire to solve some of the world's thorniest problems. After some hesitation, I sensed an opening and proposed an idea, "What if we actually *invested* in the advancement of women?"

The table grew quiet. "Imagine if we invested in companies with diverse boards," I said. "What if we created new capital sources for women entrepreneurs, or funded education for girls in emerging markets?"

I had made my case, to nods all around the table. The market, we knew, might serve as a powerful lever for change. Everyone was inspired. "I love the idea," said a friend I will call Caroline. She paused. "But honestly, Andrea, I do not have time to tackle even the basics. I am embarrassed to admit this but I have three years of compensation sitting in cash."

Another friend piped up. "Even though I have met with several potential financial advisors, I just can't find one that I trust," she said. "They cold-call me after I've gotten a promotion that's made the press, a strategy I find extremely off-putting." One after another, my colleagues chimed in with stories of similar challenges in managing their own finances.

After lunch I reflected on our conversation, marveling at the irony. We had weathered grueling years climbing the ranks at our firms; we had survived the 2008 downturn; we'd become financially independent with autonomy over decisions about our careers and families—only to hit a plateau in the long-term management of our own wealth and impact. The nest eggs we had worked so hard to accumulate were stagnant. Why were we not leveraging our earnings at the same pace as our male peers? I was deeply perplexed by our collective paralysis, given what it had taken to attain this economic power.

FINANCIAL INDEPENDENCE:
A MEANS TO AN END

I grew up in the heart of Illinois, surrounded by rich farmland as far as the eye could see. Indeed, agriculture and education are at the center of my heritage—both my grandmothers went from their family farms to college in the midst of the Great Depression.

They passed that passion for education to both of my parents. My father, in particular, strongly wanted his children to attend the best universities possible, no matter the cost. He wanted us to be exposed to a world outside of our small town. My mother, a teacher, wanted this too, but worried deeply about our family finances. I can remember the concern that crept over her face when the subject would come up at the dinner table. Despite her razor-sharp intuition, she struggled, as many women do, to influence our family's spending decisions, let alone investment decisions.

Observing my parents' dynamic, and their difficulty to fund their aspirations for their family, I became determined to secure my own financial independence. I never wanted to worry about paying for college tuition for my children. I never wanted a lack of financial acumen or confidence to impede my own voice at the decision-making table.

While I did not know much about it, a career in investment banking seemed an obvious way to ensure both financial independence and acumen. So, with graduation approaching, I applied for jobs on Wall

Street. I quickly acquired the thick skin I'd need to succeed during my first interview for an investment banking analyst role. Halfway through discussing my academic background with a senior leader at the firm, he stopped me mid-sentence, and said, "Now you are a pretty young girl. Why would you want a job in investment banking when you'll just end up married with kids in a few years?"

My jaw dropped. No mock interview had prepared me for this moment. As tactfully as I could, I told him his question was irrelevant to a conversation about my credentials. I wish I had stopped there. But I was so embarrassed, I continued talking and assured him that, regardless, I had no intention of starting a family in the foreseeable future, and that I didn't even have a boyfriend at the time.

I survived the interview circuit, secured my first analyst position, and for several years, put in 90-hour workweeks. To hone my leadership and management skills, I enrolled in the Columbia Business School MBA program. There, my aspirations started to change. I studied social enterprise and earned a master's degree in international relations. I connected with mentors who broadened my worldview, professors and practitioners who inspired me. One of them was Bruce Usher, CEO of Eco Securities, a pioneer in the burgeoning carbon finance industry; as an adjunct he taught one of Columbia's most popular courses: Finance & Sustainability. He practiced what he preached: in

2009, after going public, Eco Securities was acquired by JPMorgan Chase. Bruce's inclusive teaching style and his ability to construct a flourishing career rooted in his values, planted a seed that I, too, could aspire to more than personal security for my family.

By my mid-thirties, I had the career on Wall Street that my 18-year-old self had envisioned. Certainly I had the acumen and the independence. But something was missing. I couldn't pinpoint it at first. I tried running marathons; I travelled to Tanzania and Cambodia. Gradually, however, I realized what it was: I saw no one around me I wished to emulate. The values of my profession were entirely about performance, status, and the bottom-line. Men and women who might serve as mentors lacked that inspirational quality I saw in Bruce Usher during graduate school. They seemed to have sacrificed a great deal to fit the cultural mold. No one had harnessed, as Usher had, his or her intellectual might and financial power to drive an agenda larger than his/her own remuneration.

A MAD MEN WORLD

Even before I got married, I'd begun looking for a financial advisor, turning to my friends and colleagues for referrals. I didn't succeed. Women I deeply respected and admired would tell me, "I don't have an advisor," or, "I'm not happy with my advisor, so I wouldn't recommend him." But once we were married, I was determined we find one. Since my peers had no one to suggest, we turned to my husband's male colleagues. They gave us several names, and so we started courting them to find our match.

The first advisor we met with sent me right back to my first job interview. Because my husband also worked on Wall Street, this advisor directed all of his questions to him, not once looking at me. He ran through a list of discovery questions about our finances, family structure, and short-term goals, but never asked about our individual or joint aspirations. We moved on, working our way down the list of names, only to find this *Mad Men* encounter repeated. My husband was as baffled as I was by the 1950s stereotypical approach and salesmanship. No one probed our spending habits in relation to our financial values and goals, let alone offered the solutions that had inspired me in graduate school.

So by the time I sat down to lunch with my female peers in the summer of 2011, my frustration had annealed into something of a mission. As women—as wealth creators and leaders—we had the financial know-how and the will to harness our wealth to drive social change. We needed only to find partners committed to our vision, advisors who could steer us to investment decisions that accomplished it.

That they proved so hard to find suggested both a market failure—and an incredible market opportunity.

THE OPPORTUNITY

The fact that women are the world's fastest-growing segment of wealth creators and controllers is not lost on the financial services industry. For the past decade, industry players have sought to measure and map this expanding segment of the wealth market. In 2010, Boston Consulting Group affirmed in its *Leveling the Playing Field* study that the female market was huge and growing—at an impressive rate of 16% in 2009, in the midst of the global recession.[1] Similarly Merrill Lynch found in 2011 that the high-net-worth women's share of the wealth market had risen by more than a tenth between 2008 and 2010.[2] Goldman Sachs, focusing on the middle class in emerging markets, demonstrated that women are making more household financial decisions, particularly when it comes to consumer goods.[3] A Citi report documented the rapid rise of female financial decision makers: between 2008 and 2010, the percentage of full-time working women who consider themselves "household Chief Financial Officer" grew from 68 to 73.[4] A Barclays study considered behaviors of wealthy women in different regions around the globe, stopping short of explaining how geographic and other factors affect the way they approach financial planning.[5] In one of the most comprehensive studies of women and wealth, BlackRock affirmed in a 2013 study that women were more likely than men to save and pay off debt, but were also more conservative and less confident investors than men.[6]

From these multiple studies, a profile of the female wealth market emerged. But it's a frustratingly monolithic market that's portrayed. Women vary depending on where they live, how old they are, whether they're married or not, and whether they're earning income or in charge of managing it. What wealth managers needed, I realized, was a more nuanced picture, with data that not only quantified women's untapped wealth but also laid bare their unmet needs and gave voice to their desires in terms of services and products.

And I had an idea where to get it. While pursuing my master's at Columbia, I had the good fortune to work with Sylvia Ann Hewlett, a Cambridge-educated economist whose think tank, the Center for Talent Innovation, was working on advancing women in the ranks of Fortune 500 companies like the banks I'd worked for. Sylvia had approached me to help her create an index to rate companies on the basis of their diversity in leadership.

I shared with her my observation about women, who in my experience not only wanted to work for companies committed to diversity, but to invest in them as well—to invest in alignment with their values and to amplify their agency. Sylvia immediately got it: the Center had just concluded research that quantified the impact of leveraging diverse talent to drive innovation and capture new markets. To their credit, several corporate partners (Deutsche Bank, Credit Suisse, Goldman Sachs, Morgan Stanley, Standard Chartered, and UBS) also got it, providing the resources needed to fund our project and connect us to many forward-thinking advisors and executives who'd given considerable thought to strategies that might capture the female market worldwide.

In 2013, she and I embarked on our research. With the research team at the Center, we surveyed nearly 6,000 investors with at least $500,000 of investible assets or $100,000 of income in the United States, United Kingdom, India, China, Hong Kong, and Singapore. In May of 2014, the Center published our findings in *Harnessing the Power of the Purse: Female Investors and Global Opportunities for Growth*, a report that quantifies the market opportunity that women represent. It details how women differ, not only from men but from each other. It makes clear how culture, generation, and sources of wealth (inherited or self-created) impact women's investment approach. It lays bare what women want from wealth, and how they make decisions regarding its allocation and deployment. It measures women's confidence, financial savvy, and risk aversion, testing presumptions that women are less financially literate and less risk tolerant—and if so, under what conditions. And it spells out what women want from wealth managers, and what advisors and the industry need to do to win their trust and loyalty.

A WAY FORWARD FOR WOMEN, WEALTH MANAGERS, AND THE INDUSTRY

This book takes our report one step further: it lays out strategies for advisors and institutions to leverage women's wealth. Our research demonstrates that, in order to harness the power of the purse, change must happen at two levels: in the culture of firms, and in the behaviors of advisors on the frontlines with clients.

You will hear from men and women in the industry who are implementing innovative solutions—advisors and firm leaders who have learned to listen to women and offer differentiated client experiences that align women's investments with their goals, their aspirations, and their values. You'll meet industry leaders who are forging the kind of culture where female advisors can thrive and contribute their insights, deepening the pipeline of ideas that culminate in innovation for female investors. You'll come to see how inclusive leaders and gender-smart advisors build successful businesses by driving market growth in ways that benefit us all, from boosting educational access to building trust with clients, from launching vehicles that invest in diversity to helping clients thrive wherever they live.

With this research, I've come to see my own meaning and purpose as a wealth creator: to connect the industry to its most powerful market, and to use the market to realize women's most cherished goals. On that afternoon in 2011, my women colleagues and I enumerated a vision for the enriched world we wanted to create, a world where we could strike a balance between the bottom-line, enhance the lives of our families, and have a positive impact on society. I hope this book ignites a transformation for women investors, advisors, and the industry—and that it inspires you to be part of this virtuous cycle.

PART ONE
THE MARKET

1

The Purse

The power of the purse is mighty—and growing. Women control $20 trillion, or about 27% of the world's wealth.[7] They're the purse-string holders throughout the developed world: women account for 85% of all consumer purchases in the US, from personal computers to pharmaceuticals, from bank accounts to new homes.[8] In developing markets as well, women control spending, with 73% in China and 69% in India saying they allocate household resources for their families.[9]

But women don't merely control the purse: they're filling it. As 40% of the global labor force,[10] women already earn an estimated $13 trillion worldwide.[11] Women own or operate, according to World Bank estimates, between 25% and 33% of all private business globally.[12] In the US, women own eight million businesses, with an annual economic impact of nearly $3 trillion.[13] If American women-owned businesses made up a country, it would be the fifth largest GDP in the world, ahead of the UK and France.[14] Every year, more women join the ranks of the world's wealthiest, with a record-breaking 172 women on Forbes' Billionaires list in 2014, up from 138; 12% of the newcomers are women who created their own wealth.[15] Nearly 21% of Financial Times Stock Exchange (FTSE) 100 board seats[16] and 17.6% of Fortune 500 executive officer positions, are now held by women.[17]

Women are increasingly likely, we find, to be their household's primary breadwinner. Our data shows that among college-educated women between the ages of 21 and 64 working full-time in white-collar professions, 52% out-earn their spouse or partner. Fully 68%—of women we surveyed in China and 68% in Hong Kong report that income from their business and/or compensation from their employment represents their household's primary source of assets.

Women are, in short, economic powerhouses: they are not just influencing wealth, but dictating its deployment. In the US alone, we find women exercise either primary or joint decision-making control over a purse worth $11.2 trillion. That's a whopping 39% of the nation's $28.6 trillion total investable assets. And nearly half of that purse—$5.1 trillion—is managed solely by women.

Figure 1.1
Proportion of women (out of all women and men) who are decision makers
over assets in the US*

Total: 28.6 trillion†

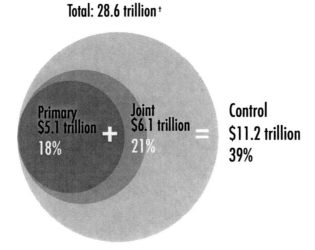

Primary
$5.1 trillion
18%

+

Joint
$6.1 trillion
21%

=

Control
$11.2 trillion
39%

* Decision-making status was computed by aggregating the number of female respondents who are primary (joint)
decision makers over assets held in their name, assets held jointly, or assets held in someone else's name and
dividing by the total number of respondents (men and women). This proportion is weighted by the amount of assets
that respondents are primary (joint) decision makers over relative to the total amount of their household assets.
Sample includes people who make at least $100,000 annually or have at least $500,000 in investable assets.

† Federal Reserve Flow of Funds Report, 10/4/11-3/12/09, Tiburon Research & Analysis.

While we cannot extrapolate the size of the purse in
other countries, we do know from our global sample
that, on average, 66% of women describe themselves
as a household decision maker. Wealth creators are the
most likely to describe themselves as decision makers
(as fully 75% do), but surprisingly, so too do 66% of
inheritors and 43% of women whose spouses created
their wealth. Women in Asia wield the most power: 87%
of women in China and 71% of women in Hong Kong

say that they are decision makers; in India, 80% of women are in charge of household assets.

Figure 1.2
Proportion of women (out of all women) who are decision makers over household assets*

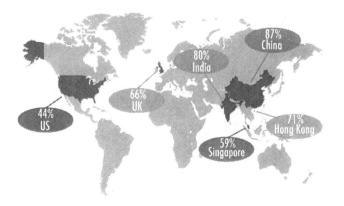

* Decision-making status was computed by aggregating the number of female respondents who are primary (joint) decision makers over assets held in their name, assets held jointly, or assets held in someone else's name and dividing by the total number of women respondents. This proportion is weighted by the amount of assets that respondents are primary (joint) decision makers over relative to the total amount of their household assets. Sample includes people who make at least $100,000 annually or have at least $500,000 in investable assets.

This trend persists even when we segment the global female investor pool by wealth level and age. Fully 63% of women in our global sample with under $1 million in assets exercise control over those assets, as do 73% of women with at least $1 million in assets—and as do 56% of women who are 40 years of age or older.[18]

DEEPENING THE BUSINESS CASE

As decision makers over a sizeable purse, women represent a market that wealth managers and advisors can ill afford to overlook. But because women are wage earners and wealth creators, the purse—and the market opportunity—is growing. Compounding the wealth that women generate is the wealth they will inherit: research conducted at Boston College's Center on Wealth and Philanthropy estimated that some $41 trillion will change hands by 2055 as Americans pass their assets from one generation to the next.[19] In the greater Boston area, for example, it is expected that nearly 63% of the final estates will be in the hands of women by 2055.[20] Little wonder that the majority of women we surveyed describe their financial situation as "increasing in assets." The outlook is particularly rosy in Asia, where more than 75% of female wealth creators in India and China say their assets are increasing. Not coincidentally, nearly 20% the world's richest self-made women are Chinese.[21] As we'll see in Chapter 6, these women represent the leading edge of the female wealth market.

Indeed, the most remarkable finding to emerge from our inquiry is that the purse is vast and growing because women are increasingly generating, and not just dispensing, its contents. They're women like Laurie Ann Goldman, former CEO of Spanx, the shapewear behemoth, who started her journey up the

Figure 1.3
How would you describe your current financial situation: Increasing assets
(Women by wealth source)

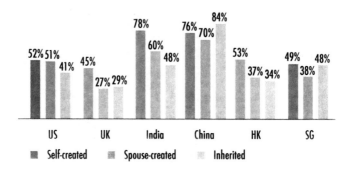

Figure 1.4
What is the primary source of your household assets?
(Women by wealth source)

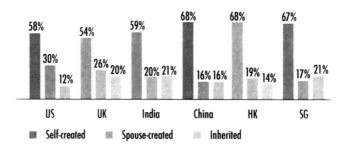

ladder—as chairman of Coca-Cola prior to Spanx—
at her childhood dinner table where she used to
compete in a family quiz show.[22] They're women like
Peggy Yu, cofounder of dangdang.com, the largest
online retailer in China.[23] They're women like Helena
Morrissey, CEO of Newton Investments, who oversees
a portfolio of some £55 billion.[24] And they're women
like Megan Ellison, who, while set to inherit some of
her father's $50.3 billion (Oracle founder Larry Ellison's
net worth in April 2014),[25] has leveraged her wealth to
create and run Annapurna Pictures, a film production
and distribution company with two of its 2013 pictures
nominated for multiple Academy Awards.[26]

These are women for whom leveraging wealth is
important, not merely to assure them and their loved
ones of financial security, but also to empower them as
change agents. They work hard and dream big. And to
achieve their goals and realize their larger agenda, they
require sound advice and high-level expertise.

But whether they seek this expertise from a wealth
management professional or from the Internet, from a
family member or from a financial advisor, is largely up
to the industry to determine. To harness the power of
the purse, broker dealers, boutique firm owners, private
bankers, and wealth managers must convince women
that an advisory relationship is the best way to grow
their assets, fulfill their needs, and achieve their dreams.

As we'll see in the next chapter, that's an imperative
the industry has yet to grasp.

2

Money Left on the Table

After her father's death, Melanie,* an equity partner at a prominent professional services firm, recognized she needed a new advisor to help manage her assets. At 48, she had amassed significant wealth, enough to bump her into the high-net-worth (HNW) category of investor—a fact she found astonishing. But she had also inherited her father's estate, which was ridden with debt. And she had recently decided to take a sabbatical from her firm to explore launching a new business. In short, she wanted an advisor who could help her sort out the mess of her father's estate and put her own money to work so that she could fund her aspirations.

What happened in her subsequent meetings with prospective firms sorely tested her trust in wealth management. As a HNW prospect, Melanie says, she anticipated personal attention and a committed effort to understand her: her current situation, her near-future plans, and her long-term goals and financial needs. Instead, she was shown proposals that repeatedly failed to take into consideration what she had spelled

* pseudonym used at interviewee's request

out in terms of her near- and long-term goals: taking a sabbatical and living off of her investments while she pursued her dream job. She also found herself repeatedly forced to counter assumptions about her wealth status. "Each of the advisors with whom I met assumed that my assets were attributable to my father's estate, rather than my own hard work," says this daughter of immigrants who put herself through graduate school on a $20 weekly food budget. The last straw, she says, was when she was encouraged to reallocate some of her current investments to incorporate higher-fee in-house products. Despite having no background in finance, Melanie could see the numbers didn't add up in her favor. "I found it very insulting," she says. "They kept talking about my 'family' wealth, my philanthropic 'obligations.' It was a total disconnect."

In the end, Melanie wound up staying with her father's institution and changing her advisor. She's not particularly happy, but doesn't wish to invest any more energy shopping for the ideal relationship. "The guys I was meeting with elsewhere had a real opportunity because I was eager to work with a new institution," she notes. "But they didn't want to listen or take the time to understand my needs."

UNTAPPED, OR TAPPED AND MISUNDERSTOOD

Female wealth isn't connecting with the wealth management industry. Many women have advisors whom they don't particularly trust or feel understand them, or they don't have advisors at all. Many women we spoke with were seeking an advisor, but struggled to find one that understood them.

The majority of female wealth in the world is, in fact, currently unmanaged. Women in Asia are the most underserved: 61% in Hong Kong, 57% in India, and 56% in Singapore say they don't have an advisor. When we segment the prospective female investor market by wealth level, age, and wealth source, certain populations emerge as particularly underserved. For example, in Hong Kong, fully 70% of female inheritors lack advisors. Fifty-three percent of female millionaires in the UK lack a financial advisor, as do 75% of women under 40 in the US. Female wealth, our data shows, is surprisingly untapped.

Figure 2.1
Do not currently have a financial advisor
(Women)

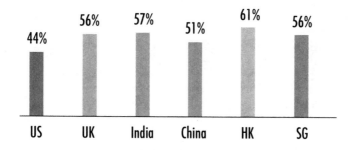

Most of those who do have an advisor, however, aren't very happy. The vast majority of our sample feel their advisor does "not understand" them. This trend holds true across all subsegments of the female market, irrespective of age and asset levels. The wealth-generating segment in Asia feels strongly misunderstood: 86% of creators in Hong Kong, 83% of creators in Singapore, and 76% of creators in India report this disconnect. The under 40 segment and women with over $1 million of assets feel particularly misunderstood in the US (where 72% and 51% feel their advisor is out of touch). And women who inherit from their husbands are also dissatisfied, at least in the UK. More than 70% of widows fire their financial professionals within a year of their husband's deaths.[27]

Figure 2.2
My advisor does not understand me
(Women)

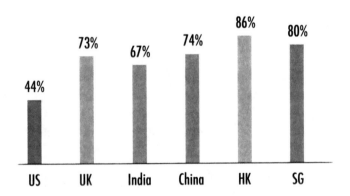

Women who do have a financial advisor seem to be opting out of traditional private bank and broker dealer models. Our data shows a strong preference among women in every country except Hong Kong and

Singapore for boutique firms, which tend to offer their clients a more holistic wealth management approach with customized planning, investments, and charitable giving strategies. In the US, women are 6.4 times more likely to work with a boutique firm than a private bank, and 61% more likely to work with a boutique firm than a broker dealer.

Figure 2.3
What type of advisor is your primary financial advisor?
(Women)

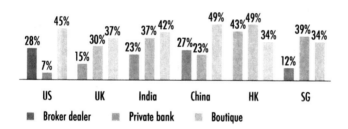

Our qualitative findings shed light on why. Focus groups and interviews we conducted in the US, the UK, and India with high-net-worth women and female investors relying on bankers and broker dealers portrayed an industry profoundly out of touch with its clients. Many complained of overt and unconscious bias. Sunita, a professor based in Mumbai, left a large international private bank because "every time I wanted to buy something or make a decision about my account our relationship manager would call my husband to make sure he knew." Jennifer, a business owner in New York, described sitting down for a first meeting with a banker and being asked, "And what does your husband do?"

But bias is the tip of the iceberg. Women do not feel, as our data exemplifies, that the industry truly understands their differentiated value proposition or the way in which they make decisions. Several high-earning women complained of being shown product-centric pitches and detailed, transaction-based spreadsheets, when what they wanted was to see a portfolio reflective of and framed by their broader life goals. Uniformly, they felt sold to rather than listened to, and pushed to make purchases rather than encouraged to articulate goals that might help them align their investment decisions with their values. "I'm sick of having performance data shoved in my face," a London professional declared. "Don't give me the sales pitch. Don't give me information that's dictated by reporting systems and regulators. Ask me the right questions— what I do, whether I have kids, what are my goals—and then come back to me with solutions you can defend."

Given the size of the purse, the disconnect women report represents trillions of dollars "left on the table" by wealth management firms. Inheritors' dissatisfaction is particularly costly: when you consider that half of women over age 65 outlive their husbands by 15 years,[28] and that these women are more likely than men to inherit the $41 trillion of wealth transferred in the US over the next 40 years,[29] then losing even a small portion of them represents an awful lot of money left on the table.

THE REAL COST OF UNLEVERAGED WEALTH

Yet it's not merely wealth management firms who pay, in lost revenues, for this failure to connect. Women, too, leave money on the table, not because they necessarily lack an advisor but because they're prone to underinvest their assets. In the US, for example, women without a financial advisor hold, on average, 20% of their portfolio in cash, whereas women with an advisor hold, on average, only nine percent in cash.[30] While keen to engage as decision makers, women often lack the confidence and know-how to fully leverage their own assets, our findings suggest. When those assets fail to grow, women's ability to transform the world is stunted.

And women are the world's change agents. According to the International Labor Organization, women represent the single most important poverty-reducing factor in developing economies.[31] Consider the stunning impact women have had as microenterprise founders and operators. Microfinance lenders like Grameen Bank and Ashoka have instigated a wave of economic empowerment in the world's most impoverished corners by empowering their borrowers—a staggering 96% of whom are women in the case of Grameen Bank—with "ownership of assets" and decision-making power of the deployment of those assets.[32]

As this book will highlight throughout, women want from their wealth an ability to enrich the world—both theirs and the world around them—by seeding new ventures, funding social enterprise, creating charitable foundations, and leveling the playing field for all in terms of access to education, employment, and capital.

So when women leave money on the table—when their assets remain unleveraged—the world, not just women and their families, goes wanting. In the next chapter, we'll unpack some of the reasons why women and wealth management struggle to join forces.

PART TWO
UNDERSTANDING THE FEMALE INVESTOR

3

What Women Want

As one of few female portfolio managers in the asset management space, Arlene* makes it her business to support women in finance. So when a former colleague in wealth management invited her to attend a launch party she was hosting for her new advisory firm, Arlene agreed to join the guest list of high-networth individuals. When she arrived at New York's Guggenheim museum, she found herself navigating a crowd of older men and their bejeweled wives. Ignored by the hostess, who was intent on her male quarry, Arlene struck up a conversation with a male senior banker she knew, only to be interrupted by an older gentleman who, like the hostess, was intent on building his book of business. Casting a dismissive eye at Arlene, he introduced himself to the senior banker. Her banker friend, amused, leaned in to whisper to her, "Oh, if only he knew how much working wealth you have, Arlene."

Arlene, who manages a $5 billion portfolio, left shortly thereafter. "It was all so terribly out of date," she says. "There was not a single person of youth or diversity in evidence, and about ten women to three

_____

hundred men. I can't imagine what my friend thinks she's doing setting up such a business. I'm certainly not going to give them any of my money."

THE BIG DIVIDE

Wealth managers, as Arlene's story illustrates and our research affirms, are wed to an out-of-date conception of who's got the money and who makes the decisions. They're inclined to recognize women as influencers over household assets, as wives who are likely to outlive their husbands, divorcees, and inheritors of family wealth. But as wealth generators or decision makers, women are barely on their radar.

Given the size of the purse, this is a costly assumption to cling to. As we saw in Chapter 1, women don't just control household expenditures, they allocate family assets. Fully 66% of women we surveyed exercise decision-making control over investable assets, versus 81% of men. And women are increasingly, like Arlene, wealth generators, not just spouses or inheritors. They want to be taken seriously as investors, granted agency in their relationships with advisors, and to have their value recognized.

Some wealth managers targeting female investors, such as Jamie Broderick, CEO of UK wealth management at UBS, well understand that the female market is evolving. "The mistake we don't want to make is to treat a female industry leader in a certain way because she is a woman; we need to focus on addressing her needs as an investor," he says. But in other ways wealth managers fail to grasp that the female market is highly nuanced. "There's no one 'she-conomy,'" a boutique banker observed in our London focus group. "Women in Southeast Asia want different things from their wealth than women in, say, Europe, and younger women behave very differently from older women."

Figure 3.1
Decision makers over household assets
(US, UK, India, China, Hong Kong, and Singapore)

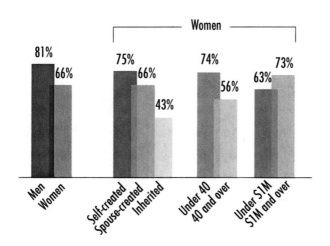

Indeed, our survey findings bear this out: geography, generation, wealth level, and source of wealth nuance the female market. Women who create their wealth want different things from it than spouses and inheritors, and their priorities—we uncovered six— vary depending on where they live, how old they are, and how much money they have. Wealth creators make decisions differently from wives and widows, certainly, but also from each other, depending on their age and locale. Confidence and financial literacy levels vary wildly, not just between Asian, European, and American women but also Gen Xers and Boomers, millionaires and aspiring millionaires. Women are widely perceived by the industry as risk-averse investors, but when we segment the female market (as we will see in the next three chapters), we find wide variance in risk tolerance.

Bottom line? Nuances matter in capturing the female market. Just as it would be a mistake to treat female prospects merely as influencers, so too would it be a mistake to treat women as a monolithic market.

WHAT WOMEN WANT FROM WEALTH

In one very important respect, women of all ages and stages the world over are like each other; they want to achieve personal success as well as a greater social good. Research that CTI conducted in 2014 in the US, the UK, and Germany reveals that college-educated working women between the ages of 35-50 want work to enable them to flourish, or self-actualize; to excel, and be recognized for their mastery; and to earn well, in order to provide for their families as well as their own financial independence and security. But we also find that women are more likely than men to say deriving a sense of meaning and purpose from their work is important to them. Fully 80% of our US sample of women identifies this as important, versus 70% of men surveyed in the US. Women find work particularly meaningful when it helps advance causes important to them. And while women are less likely than men to aspire to positions of power, they're utterly intent on being empowered and empowering others. They want to be sponsored, but they also want to pull up others behind them and have the influence to promote talent whom they believe to be worthy.

Understanding what women want from their careers and their lives provides a critical context for advisors and wealth managers seeking to understand what women—particularly female wealth creators—want as investors. Just as they seek ways to advance causes important to them through work, women want their wealth to promote "a greater basket of goods." They're seeking a financial plan that acknowledges their agency, aligns with their values, and makes possible their vision.

This isn't to say that women don't prioritize, as men do, financial performance. Performance is paramount to female investors across the geographies we surveyed, because it affords them the financial security and financial independence they value so highly. The vast majority of women we surveyed (88% of US women, 84% of Chinese women, and 72%, on average, of women in India, Hong Kong, and Singapore) equate wealth with security; large numbers equate wealth with financial independence, too.

Figure 3.2
Wealth means financial security
(Men vs. Women)

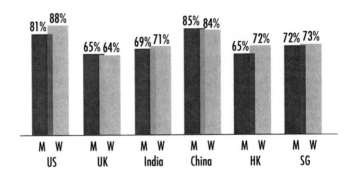

Importantly, women also want wealth to bring them latitude in their career choice. More than a third of American women under the age of 40 (creators, inheritors, and spouses) for example, are likely to see wealth in terms of the career choices it opens up for them. Some 38% of the under-40 cohort say this is important, versus 16% of the 40-and-over crowd. Women are more inclined than men to perceive wealth in this way. Female wealth creators in the US, for example, are 79% more likely than male respondents to see wealth as enabling greater career choice. This trend is also particularly pronounced among female creators in the UK (who are 58% more likely than men to see wealth in terms of career options); and women under 40, who are 89% more likely than women who are at least 40 to want money to buy them career latitude.

A GREATER BASKET OF GOODS

When asked what having wealth means to them, women also cite the importance of being able to fund their aspirations and drive their agenda, which includes advancing causes that are important to them, their families, and their communities. They want both their time and their money to advance important causes, whether that's investing in their own businesses or acting as an angel investor for companies they believe in, investing in socially responsible corporations or funding microenterprises. They're donating to charities that fight poverty, or they're keen to invest in funds that aggregate socially responsible entities. Fully 90% of women in our global sample say "making a positive impact on society is important," and 88% say they want to invest in organizations that promote social well-being.

"Women want money not so much for what it can buy, but rather, for what it can do," observes former Goldman Sachs partner Jacki Zehner, who is CEO of Women Moving Millions, a network of philanthropists dedicated to improving the lives of girls and women worldwide. "They want to provide for their family but also be in the service of others."

Women, much more so than men, we find, want to invest according to their values: in the US and UK, we uncovered significant discrepancies between men's and women's desire to improve gender equality, education, and the environment by funneling resources into impact-investing and philanthropy. Ultimately they wish to grow their money in such a way as to further, rather than undermine, their goals around promoting social good. As Zehner puts it, "Why would I give five percent to specific causes if the other ninety-five percent is creating the problems I'm trying to solve for? I'm not about to enable a power structure I fundamentally don't believe in."

Women in Asia are even keener than American and European women to do good with their money. Stunning majorities of women in China (97%) and India (96%) want to invest in organizations that promote social good, as compared to 82% of women in the UK and 76% of women in the US. Even more notably, Asian men are as likely as Asian women to invest in fighting poverty, addressing gender inequality, improving education and social services, and improving the environment.

Figure 3.3
I want to invest in organizations that promote social well-being
(Men vs women)

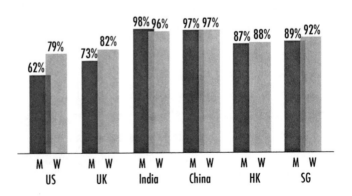

This is why harnessing women's investment power is so important: invested assets will not only grow advisor portfolios and wealth management firms, they will also accelerate progress in education, health, gender and racial equality, environmental protection, and a host of other worthy causes. When women fully leverage their wealth, everybody wins.

Yet only a tiny portion of the purse's power is being tapped. As we'll see in Chapter 4, of the 31% of US women investors who want to invest in gender equality, for example, only eight percent actually do; of the 35% who are determined to make a positive difference in the environment, 21% succeed in investing in environmentally responsible assets; and of the 28% of women who want to invest in health, a mere nine percent do so. Advisors lose out, but so too does society at large.

There's an incredible opportunity here, then, for advisors who can furnish women with products that speak to values and strategies that achieve their life goals. "I think there's a real desire to connect the values piece," Jacki Zehner says. "More and more I think people want to align their personal and philanthropic values with investing but don't know how to do that—and the marketplace hasn't shown them how to do it."

DIVERSITY MATTERS

One of the values that women across markets want their wealth to promote is greater workplace diversity, particularly in the top tiers of management. Fully 77% of women we surveyed in the global sample said they wanted to invest in companies whose leadership is diverse. This is a particularly important value for women in Asia, as 93% of Indian women, 94% of Chinese women, 88% of women in Singapore, and 83% of women in Hong Kong affirm. Interestingly, in those countries the percentages of men who put a premium on diversity are just as high.

Figure 3.4
Investors who want to invest in organizations with diversity in leadership
(Men vs women)

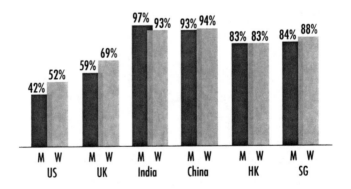

Women's emphasis on diversity can in part be explained by their intention to promote gender equality, a value articulated by many of the high-net-worth investors and asset managers we heard from in focus groups and interviews. Elaine*, a financial professional who'd been vetting money managers to determine whom she would reward with oversight of her family's 100 million-dollar foundation, recounted how one top Wall Street team engaged with her during their hour-long meeting: "I'm asking all the questions, and not once did the portfolio manager look me in the eye," she told us.

But what must be stressed is that women want more women, people of color, and people of varying social, economic, and educational backgrounds to be at the decision-making table because they perceive that a diverse team drives better performance. Elaine, for example, uses the leverage that her assets confer to make clear to wealth managers on Wall Street that without team diversity she has to question their competitive edge. "In all of my meetings—and I've been in hundreds of new business pitches—I'll ask to be introduced to the entire research team," she explains. "They'll be men, of course. So I say, 'There's not one woman on your team. I don't see how you can be good asset managers without different perspectives.' They'll respond, 'Oh, but we're aware of those perspectives, we have mothers and daughters.' And I say, 'But your mother or daughter can't get a job with you. I have a hard time believing you'll be world-class in performance without your recognizing the value of other voices.'" Elaine pushes the point because, she says, "this is about them having a broader view. At my firm, when we're in meetings, you have a bunch of people—men, women, black, white, old,

<hr/>

* pseudonym used at interviewee's request

young, Harvard MBAs, no-name MBAs sitting around the table kicking around ideas. It can get heated, but we welcome the dissension. Because you need diverse opinions to solve hard problems, to arrive at a winning portfolio. It's terribly easy to have group-think unless you insist on hearing from people unlike yourself who come at problem-solving from a different angle."

Women we interviewed emphasized that adding a few women to the front lines of wealth management doesn't address what they perceive to be a systemic issue. As one successful entrepreneur told us, "It's not, 'We hire five more women and we'll have more female accounts.' It's about creating a culture and environment of inclusion. Women perceive the difference, and will invest accordingly."

Elaine, for one, believes that a shift in mindset and culture is inevitable in the industry precisely because more and more women in positions of wealth have gotten there by earning the money themselves. "They'll ask the questions [about diversity] because like me, they've been in a million situations where men haven't even bothered to make eye contact. It's inevitable."

In the meantime, wealth managers intent on capturing the female market would do well to recognize that women don't just differ from men, in what they value and what they want from their wealth. In important ways, they differ from each other. We find critical nuances within the female market when it comes to which aspects of the "greater basket of goods" matter most. Women differ in their financial confidence, their financial literacy, and their appetite for risk, depending on their market segment. An heiress from the UK, we find, has a different investing framework and decision-making approach than an entrepreneur in China, and isn't at all similar to a single Gen X executive in the US. In the next three chapters, we'll unravel these complexities to highlight the importance of creating differentiated client experiences for women.

4

What American Women Want

After graduating Columbia Business School in 1980, Deborah Jackson worked on Wall Street, specializing in healthcare finance for government and nonprofit clients. She started at Goldman Sachs and later went to Shattuck Hammond Partners to launch its healthcare and technology practice, where she focused on software, hardware, and internet companies. "That's when I discovered my love for the power of technology," she says. "I had watched the Internet come about and saw that you could do things with it that simply couldn't have been done before."

Jackson is the founder of Plum Alley, a platform that connects women entrepreneurs with markets, capital, and advice. It launched in September 2011 as "Etsy with a twist," offering visitors carefully curated items (including special site-only editions) from women-founded, women-owned businesses, but also spotlighting the innovators themselves with in-depth profiles about how each came to bring her passion to the marketplace. "I wanted to highlight all the amazing things women are doing," says Jackson, who'd met many of the women she champions during the course of her travels in tech. "I wanted a site where you could buy beautiful products and learn about the women who made them, because their stories are so inspirational."

Plum Alley isn't Jackson's first foray into entrepreneurship. In 2011, with more time on her hands (her children were older), she launched a series of women-focused initiatives. She began with JumpThru, a subscription-based letter about women and technology. Then came Women Innovate Mobile, the first startup accelerator and mentorship-driven program designed for women-founded companies in mobile technology. "What I cared about was seeing more women found companies, use and build technology, and use their money and resources to further what they believed in," she explains. "That was my mission."

Her passion to connect female entrepreneurs and innovators to women with capital culminated, in 2013, with a crowd-funding platform on the Plum Alley site— "a kickstarter for women, by women," she explains. The site also acts as a vast professional network, connecting women entrepreneurs with expertise and insight as well as seed money. "You can tap into our network of experts—men and women—and hire those people for a specific project, as many have retired or are looking for part-time or project work just like this," she clarifies. "If you're a project creator looking for a panel of experts to hire, this is incredible added value."

With Plum Alley's success, says Jackson, she's seeing her values at work, her passions in play, and her life mission on its way to being accomplished. "It's very satisfying," she notes. "We have a brand and a community that we're building that for many women is life-changing." There's nothing she'd rather be doing, she says. "I compare this to all my years on Wall Street, and I feel, being on this side of the deal table, that I get to be the fullest person I can be."

WEALTH, MEANING, AND VALUE

As a wealth creator and social entrepreneur, Jackson typifies a new breed of female investor in the US: businesswomen who've decided to apply their hard-won capital to grant them career flexibility and help them realize their dreams. Women like Jackson want from their wealth what our research shows they want from their careers: an identity that acknowledges their vision, their values, and their agency. As outlined in the previous chapter, our earliest research on women, conducted in 2004 and repeated in 2009 and 2014, finds that women value meaningful work with high quality colleagues, the ability to earn well, and an opportunity to empower others and be empowered themselves in their careers.

INVESTOR SNAPSHOT

**(WOMEN WITH $1 MILLION OR MORE
IN ASSETS HELD IN THEIR NAME)**

AN UNTAPPED MARKET

30% don't have an advisor
51% with advisors feel misunderstood
63% are decision makers over
household assets

"WEALTH MEANS TO ME..."

90% financial security
76% financial independence
33% funding my aspirations, driving my agenda
17% greater career latitude
12% a more luxurious lifestyle

DECISION-MAKING FACTORS

30% feel confident in their financial acumen
45% are financially literate
22% perceive themselves as risk-averse
35% are risk-averse

VALUES AGENDA

74% want to invest in organizations that
promote social well-being

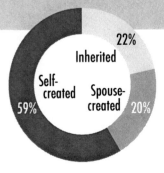

22% Inherited
Self-created 59%
Spouse-created 20%

One need only glance at the headlines to see these trends affirmed. Melinda Gates is a Boomer who, after a career at Microsoft, parlayed her joint wealth with husband Bill into the Gates Foundation, an entity that is making a profound dent in intractable problems like poverty, malaria, and education in the developing world. As the foundation's cochair and public face, she is working on issues important to her based on her Jesuit-influenced upbringing. Gen Xer Sheryl Sandberg is leveraging her worldwide visibility, professional network, and wealth to advance women's empowerment across industries. Twenty-nine-year-old Liesel Pritzker Simmons, who inherited some $300 million after suing members of her family for misappropriating trust funds based on the family's Hyatt Hotels fortune, is the cofounder and president of the IDP Foundation, a grant-making nonprofit that funds innovative education initiatives. The child actress and film star has also been active in microfinance, founding Young Ambassadors for Opportunity and donating millions to Opportunity International to extend credit to microenterprises in Africa. She sees herself as emblematic of the millennials, people under 34 who embrace a social agenda in everything they do. "This generation is thinking of different vehicles, using media and for-profit investments to further their causes," she says. "We are not all Paris Hilton, lounging on yachts in the Riviera, squandering our responsibility."[33]

WHAT DOES HAVING WEALTH MEAN TO YOU? (US)

Figure 4.1
By gender

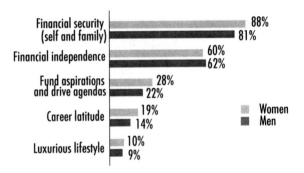

Financial security (self and family) Women 88% Men 81%
Financial independence Women 60% Men 62%
Fund aspirations and drive agendas Women 28% Men 22%
Career latitude Women 19% Men 14%
Luxurious lifestyle Women 10% Men 9%

Women
Men

Figure 4.2
Women by wealth source

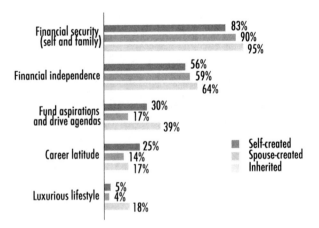

Financial security (self and family) Self-created 83% Spouse-created 90% Inherited 95%
Financial independence Self-created 56% Spouse-created 59% Inherited 64%
Fund aspirations and drive agendas Self-created 30% Spouse-created 17% Inherited 39%
Career latitude Self-created 25% Spouse-created 14% Inherited 17%
Luxurious lifestyle Self-created 5% Spouse-created 4% Inherited 18%

Self-created
Spouse-created
Inherited

Figure 4.3
Women by age

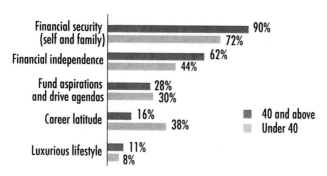

Figure 4.4
Women by wealth level

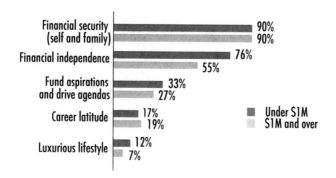

These women, with their emphasis on building an enriched world through philanthropy and social entrepreneurship, are reshaping the landscape of wealth management in the US. They define wealth differently than men; they're financially literate, though not commensurately confident; and they're less risk-averse than is commonly assumed. They're accustomed to making decisions, and intent on making the right ones with regard to their finances so that they can continue to have the means to further their causes. But given their extraordinary range of commitments—career, family, community, philanthropy—they're also desperately short on time. For wealth managers and advisors attuned to their needs, they represent an extraordinary opportunity.

Meeting that challenge requires understanding how American women arrive at financial decisions—a process influenced by factors such as confidence, knowledge, aversion to risk, and time spent.

CONFIDENCE AND LITERACY

Women in the US are knowledgeable about finance. They're virtually as knowledgeable as men (35% of women and 39% of men, passed our literacy assessment). Indeed, they're among the most financially literate investors in the world. Interestingly, however, superior knowledge does not translate into commensurate confidence: these women don't *perceive* themselves as financially literate. They're the most literate and the least confident of all the women we surveyed globally. Certainly they're far less confident than men, who are 79% more likely to express confidence in their financial know-how.

While confidence relative to acumen is low for US women overall, it's astonishingly low for certain subsectors of the female market. Wealth creators are the most literate (47%) segment, and yet only 23% of these women feel financially confident. While 34% of women with spouse-created wealth are literate, a paltry nine percent feel knowledgeable. Among the under-40 cohort, 28% are literate and 14% are confident, and among the under-$1 million in assets investor group, 33% are literate and 16% are confident.

Figure 4.5
Confidence vs. literacy*
(US)

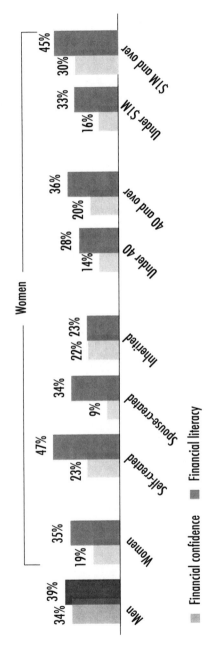

Women

■ Financial confidence ■ Financial literacy

* "Financially confident" is based on Likert-scale responses to the question "How would you rate your level of financial knowledge". "Financially literate" is based on whether respondents answered the following five questions correctly: (1) True or false: Buying a single company's stock usually provides a safer return than a stock mutual fund. (True, False); (2) Suppose you have $100 in a savings account earning 2 percent interest a year. After five years, how much would you have? (More than $102, Exactly $102, Less than $102); (3) If interest rates rise, what will typically happen to bond prices? (Rise, Fall, Stay the same, There's no relationship to bond price and interest rates); (4) Imagine that the interest rate on your savings account was 1% per year and inflation was 2% per year. After 1 year, would your money be able to buy...? (More than it does today, Exactly the same as it does today; Less than it does today); (5) True or false: A 15-year mortgage typically requires higher monthly payments than a 30-year mortgage but the total interest over the life of the loan will be less (True, False); (6) Which of the following worst-case scenario risks are possible when making investments? (You can lose the entire amount you invested in stocks, and you can lose more than the amount you invested in real estate, Losses are limited to 20% on stock and real estate investments, so if you invest $1,000 the most you can lose is $200, Your real estate investment is not liquid and you cannot sell it, Your stock investment loses all its value overnight because of what's happening in a small country on the other side of the world. Answers "a," "c" and "d").

Low confidence may play a role in women's historically low tolerance for risk. We do find, as have previous studies, that women's overall profiles are more risk-averse than men (36% of women we sampled versus 28% of men we sampled). Within the subsegments of the market, however, we find meaningful differences. Looking at the level of wealth and generational cross-sections, the most risk-averse are women with spouse-created wealth; the least risk-averse are female inheritors. Surprisingly, female inheritors turn out to be less risk-averse than men. But men's tolerance for risk turns out to be exaggerated, our research shows. Very few *perceive* themselves to be risk-averse (13%), but in fact more than twice that number (28%) opt for the most conservative of our portfolio choices.

Our data suggests that women are just more honest about their preferences. "In my experience women tend to be more thoughtful in assessing risk, which may come across as aversion," says Nicole Pullen Ross, head of the private wealth management mid-Atlantic region at Goldman Sachs. "But when they feel they understand risk, they're more comfortable embracing it. It would be a mistake to assume, based on gender stereotypes, that women just aren't in the market for complex investments or advice." Indeed, as shall be made clear in subsequent chapters, women's risk tolerance varies considerably across geography and other subsegments of the female market. Advisors who presume all women to be risk-averse only serve to underscore how poorly they understand the female market.

Figure 4.6
Perceived vs. actual risk appetite*
(US)

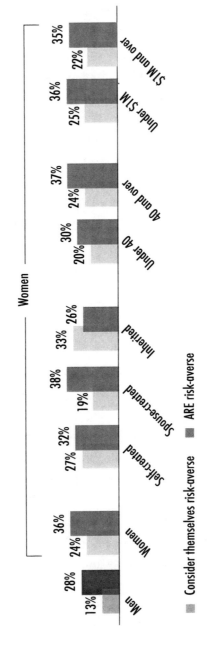

Women

| | Consider themselves risk-averse | ARE risk-averse |

* "Consider themselves risk-averse" is derived from responses to the question "Do you consider yourself…" with Likert scale responses spanning "Extremely" to "Not at all" risk-averse. "ARE risk-averse" is based on the question "Which of these investment options would you like to own?" with responses ranging from "Very risky" to "Somewhat risky" to "Not at all risky." We denoted those who picked the least risky option as risk-averse.

Still, given their incredible accomplishments as business women and entrepreneurs, and their track record as decision makers and risk takers, it's curious that American women feel so tentative about their financial savvy. It may be, as Jacki Zehner has observed, that the markets in the US are incredibly complex. "There's a ton of options to get a handle on, and so much information that you're always conscious you could know more and probably should," she says. "Expectations are definitely high, and the bar keeps rising."

Subha Barry, a consultant with decades' experience in wealth management at Merrill Lynch, observes that Asian women do not struggle, as Western women often do, with deeply engrained cultural mores that dictate men, not women, take charge of major financial decisions. Sallie Krawcheck, chair of Ellevate Network and fund principal of Ellevate Asset Management, as well as the first woman to head up global wealth management at SmithBarney and subsequently to head up wealth management at Bank of America, posits that it's time, or rather, a desperate lack of it, that undermines their engagement. "Precisely because women are so busy on so many fronts," she says, "they see wealth management and financial planning as one more thing on their plates," rather than a foundational lever to realizing greater autonomy, career flexibility, social entrepreneurship, and any number of other goals and aspirations they wish to achieve.

Our survey data corroborates this: American women spend only 5.4 hours per month, or 39% less time than men, working on their finances. Female inheritors spend more time than creators (6.2 hours per month, versus 5.9), but overall, women in the US spend less time than women in other parts of the world—significantly less time than women in India, China, and Hong Kong.

"Given the manifold claims on the time of a high-powered (and high-earning) working woman in the US," Krawcheck continues, "it's hard to put investing at the top of their to-do list. High-powered men have more discretionary time, more leisure to spend, as they are more likely to have stay-at-home spouses tending to the home front." Among the most remiss, she says, are women who are working in finance ("how ironic is that?" she parries), although Silicon Valley has its share of savvy dealmakers who likewise can't find the time to deal with their portfolio.

"Let's be honest," she concludes. "We have more than our share of extreme-job professionals who feel obliged to be extreme parents, too, and yet we're also the least likely group of women in the world to have shoulders to lean on." Well-heeled professional women in emerging markets, she notes, often have the support structure to enable them to work 65-hour weeks, manage their money, and never have to worry about childcare or domestic burdens.

Krawcheck's insights point to some instant remedies: to better serve female investors, wealth managers and advisors should strive to close the confidence gap by providing more digestible information that's packaged to address women's decision-making tendencies and which speaks to their priorities.

AN EMPHASIS ON ALTRUISM

If women's lack of time translates into a lack of confidence, we find that low confidence in turn impacts how women behave with regard to value investing and philanthropy. The less confident they are, the larger the gap we see between desire and action—between what they say they want to invest in or donate to, and what they actually put money into.

Our data surfaces a correlation between women's confidence and their values-based investing: the more confident the woman, the more likely she is to make socially conscientious investments in-line with her desires. There is less discrepancy, that is, between what women say they want to allocate, and what they actually allocate, when they're confident investors. It's possible that the discrepancy can be otherwise accounted for; it may be, for example, that women don't allocate not because they lack confidence in their acumen but because they lack assets to give away. But it's tempting to infer that helping women become more confident investors might translate into a significant economic force for social good.

Figure 4.7
Impact investing: Desire vs. commitment
(US women)

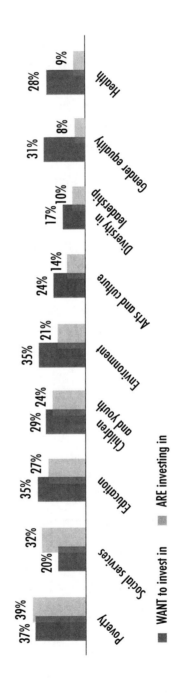

Poverty 37% 39%

Social services 32% 20%

Education 35% 27%

Children and youth 29% 24%

Environment 35% 21%

Arts and culture 24% 14%

Diversity in leadership 17% 10%

Gender equality 31% 8%

Health 28% 9%

■ WANT to invest in   ▨ ARE investing in

Our US data shows 84% of women and 71% of men are interested in making a positive impact on society. Eighty-two percent of women and 73% of men are interested in investing in organizations that align with their own goals. And 79% of women versus 62% of men want to invest in organizations that invest in social good. Altruism is a value, that is, that both men and women hold dear. Where men and women differ is in their allocation: women are 48% more likely than men (37% versus 25%) to want to invest in alleviating poverty, and twice (38% versus 19%) as likely to want to donate to poverty-fighting charities. Education is another vital cause for women. They're 88% more likely than men (30% versus 16%) to want to donate to educational charities and 46% more likely than men (35% versus 24%) to want to invest in initiatives that improve education or access to it. Finally, improving the environment is a top priority for women: they're 32% more likely than men (25% versus 19%) to want to donate, and 25% more inclined than men (35% versus 28%) to want to invest in this agenda. We find that social-impact investing resonates in particular with Gen Y women and inheritors, as Pritzker Simmons exemplifies. She has devoted time to teaching yoga to drug addicts in northern India and helping women with cottage industries in Tanzania. In 2008, she kickstarted IDP with $50 million of her own fortune to fund Karibu Homes, an affordable housing developer in Nairobi, and EcoPost, a nascent Kenyan company that turns plastic into fence posts.[34]

CHALLENGES—BUT ALSO OPPORTUNITIES FOR ADVISORS

When we unpack the female US investor, we find a complex and yet eerily familiar picture. Women yearn to make a difference in their careers; likewise women yearn to use their wealth to make a difference. They hunger for opportunity: our data on women's career drive and commitment shows robust ambition, not only in the US but in the UK, India, China, and Brazil. They want the next job; they want a position of influence. But they don't want power *over* others; they want power *to help* others. Hence our data also reveals a persistent ambivalence among highly capable, accomplished women, an ambivalence about power that makes them hover on the threshold of the C-suite and resist claiming their agency. They're knowledgeable and capable, but they're not confident in their knowledge or capability—a lack of confidence that holds them back from the leadership positions that would grant them the means to realize their most cherished goals. Only when women have sponsors—advocates who believe in their potential, go out on a limb to serve up opportunities, and push them to embrace stretch assignments and bold opportunities—do we see capable women reach for leadership and find the agency they seek.

Our data on US women's astoundingly low confidence, despite their superior financial savvy, suggests a parallel be drawn. Advisors, like sponsors, might adopt an approach that helps women see wealth as agency, as a means to important ends, and therefore as warranting their time and commitment. Advisors, like sponsors, might help women better understand themselves, not just in terms of the knowledge they have and the risk they can tolerate, but the larger life goals they hope to achieve. Women aren't averse to hard work, as our data on their career trajectories can attest; they're not afraid of complexity, either. But they will need their advisors to fill a sponsor-like role, educating them on their knowledge gaps, showing them opportunities to advance their goals.

A number of wealth advisors, creators, and philanthropists whom we interviewed had opinions on this. Closing the confidence gap, most agree, will depend on the degree to which advisors can educate women, as opposed to assailing them with jargon and passing along product literature that undermines their confidence in their literacy. "People want simple solutions," says Zehner. "They just want their money to earn a respectable return. Instead, they're pitched complex products with a doctor-like, 'Just trust us' wrapping."

As we'll see in Chapter 9, wealth advisory firms have a unique opportunity to win over the Deborah Jacksons of the nation by recognizing how their needs differ from men's. Advisors who give women a safe place to learn, share expertise and knowledge to compensate for their lack of time, and serve up products that align with their larger need to deploy wealth in socially responsible ways are likely to tap into the extraordinary power of the US purse.

5

What British Women Want

Fiona Cruickshank was 41 when she sold, in 2008, a business she'd cofounded in 1999 for £21 million. "I didn't think it would actually sell," she recalls of The Specials Laboratory, then the UK's largest manufacturer of unlicensed medicines. "I went home and looked at my bank account and thought, 'What am I going to do with this money?'"

The corporate advisor who'd helped her close the deal pointed her to a private wealth management firm—"a standard brand you'd be comfortable with," as she puts it. She stayed with the firm for three years before deciding she deserved more service and less condescension. "There wasn't a cultural fit," she explains. "They were pleased to see me because I had money. But I'm not *from* money, so I neither felt like an important client nor did I feel they understood my value proposition as an investor."

INVESTOR SNAPSHOT

(WOMEN WITH $1 MILLION OR MORE IN ASSETS HELD IN THEIR NAME)

AN UNTAPPED MARKET

53% don't have an advisor
72% with advisors feel misunderstood
71% are decision makers over household assets

"WEALTH MEANS TO ME..."

59% financial security
54% financial independence
37% funding my aspirations, driving my agenda
27% greater career latitude
18% a more luxurious lifestyle

DECISION-MAKING FACTORS

49% feel confident in their financial acumen
32% perceive themselves as risk-averse
35% are risk-averse

VALUES AGENDA

76% want to invest in organizations that promote social well-being

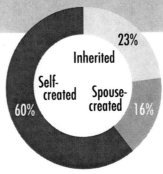

23% Inherited
60% Self-created
16% Spouse-created

While Cruickshank wanted help tending her nest egg, she also wanted to "stay in the game"—to help other start-ups in the technical and biomedical sciences space. That passion got her introduced to Anna Sofat, founder of Addidi, a boutique firm intent on providing professional women with not just investment advisory and wealth management services but access to a circle of like-minded women intent on using their wealth to give women-owned businesses and female entrepreneurs the capital and connections requisite to success. Cruickshank became one of Addidi's 30 angels, who together have pumped more than £1 million into small enterprises.

Angel investing isn't where Cruickshank looks to make significant returns. She recognizes it's a smaller, and riskier portion of her overall portfolio. But it allows her to play as an investor where she's most passionate. As with her charitable giving strategy, which Sofat also helped her create, it allows her to have ongoing impact in alignment with her values. "Having more money allows me to give away more," she explains. "Having a business background, I want to keep angel investing—it's good for women's business and it keeps my brain going. What I don't want to do is track my stock investments on a daily basis. Anna does that for me, which frees me up to focus on the longer-term view."

A MISALIGNED MARKET

Women like Cruickshank are shaking up the wealth management industry in Great Britain. While the inheritor segment of this market is stronger than in other countries we surveyed (inheritors make up 20% of female respondents in the UK), fully 73% of women we surveyed reported they create their own wealth and act as decision makers over their assets.

The established UK banks, however, are slow to grapple with this shift in demographics. The old guard, according to advisors we interviewed, still focuses on inheritors, wives, widows and divorcees, most of whom fall into the ultra-high-net-worth category (over £10 million). A private wealth manager we interviewed at an established firm said her book of clients is indicative: of her 20-plus ultra-high-net-worth client base, three are female, and of these, one is the ex-wife of a hedge-fund manager, one is breaking free of a large family with a lot of assets, and one is a business owner. "The real growth is happening at the one-to-five-million-in-assets level, particularly with an influx of wealth creators," she observes. Another relationship manager we interviewed said her team similarly struggles to build a book of professional women like Cruickshank because new hires, typically men, are assessed on their technical qualifications and compliance with regulatory requirements—not, she says, their emotional intelligence. This lack of emphasis on soft skills, she posits, drives a dog-eat-dog-world mentality that alienates women as both prospective clients and employees.

Wealth creators we gathered to discuss their advisory relationships affirm these observations. Our group consisted of women both under and over the £10 million threshold; the majority came from successful professional careers, including retail, financial services, and consulting. A consistent theme was resentment at being invisible to the industry as decision makers over the deployment of significant assets. Another was dismay at being lumped together with high-net-worth women who come by their money through divorce or inheritance. Cruickshank recalls attending a women-only dinner given several years ago by her first wealth advisor, the big bank, and finding herself surrounded by older women who'd never worked outside the home. "I couldn't relate to them," she says, "yet to our host, we were clearly the same client."

Figure 5.1
Decision makers over household assets
(UK)

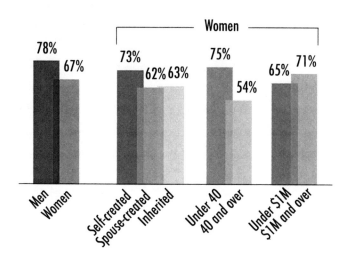

Some global banks with teams set up around entrepreneurs and the sectors in which they operate are indeed staking unclaimed territory by taking pains to discern between creators and inheritors, decision makers and influencers. Jamie Broderick, CEO of wealth management for UBS in the UK, says his team started to focus on newer wealth and in particular female wealth ten years ago because it was a sector clearly poised to expand. "I absolutely see the shift toward women as wealth creators," he says, pointing to the gains made by the Thirty Percent Club (Helena Morrissey's initiative to get London boards to up their representation of women) and the number of women heading up businesses in tech, retail, and pharma. "Inherited wealth will continue to matter and be an area of focus for us, but we don't see the same level of growth potential."

MEANING AND VALUE

These women, according to Broderick, want what their male counterparts want: performance. Our data bears this out. For both men and women, performance is baseline. So too is financial security (although it is of particular interest, predictably, for those with under $1 million in investable assets, and for those 40 years of age and older). Where men and women differ, we find, is in how else they define wealth. Men in our UK sample put a premium on financial independence: 56% of men versus 49% of women say this is what wealth means for them. So do wealth creators, who are twice as likely as inheritors (58% versus 29%) to equate wealth with independence. And surprisingly, so do spouse creators, 44% of whom see in wealth the prospect of independence; and the 40 and over crowd (57% of whom define wealth as independence, versus 44% of those under 40). "We are the first, or maybe second, generation of women for whom financial independence is incredibly important," says Helena Morrissey, CEO of Newton Investments. "We were all brought up with this goal. It's in our DNA."

More significantly, as we saw in Chapter 3, women are much more inclined than men to perceive wealth in terms of the career latitude it affords them: 27% of women versus 19% of men want money to allow them to reallocate where and how they apply their professional skills and expertise. And again, this trend is particularly pronounced among female creators. Women want wealth to buy them a nice lifestyle, too, as 20% of our sample admitted. But as we saw with American women, British women take a more holistic view of wealth, looking to it to provide them with the agency to fulfill a personal and professional ambition or to fund other women's aspirations or to have impact that goes beyond securing their children's future. Cruickshank, for example, wants her wealth to fund her son's education, but doesn't wish for him to grow up living off an inheritance. "He should make his own money," she says. "I'm only 47, and I want there to be more to my legacy than just his welfare."

WHAT DOES HAVING WEALTH MEAN TO YOU? (UK)

Figure 5.2
By gender

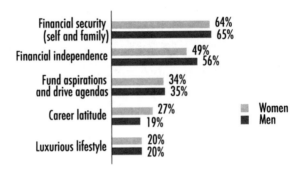

Figure 5.3
Women by wealth source

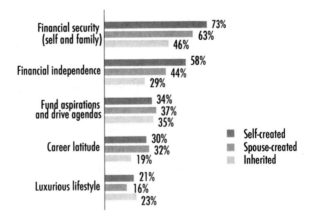

Figure 5.4
Women by age

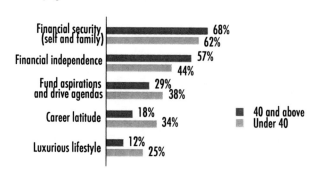

Figure 5.5
Women by wealth level

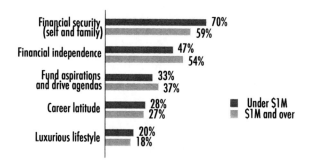

Sofat says Cruickshank is typical of her female clients in wanting more from money than a cushion. "It's all about 'personal' return," she observes. "They want to take pride in what the money has done, not in how much they've accumulated."

CONFIDENT AND RISK-TOLERANT

This new breed of female investor in the UK exhibits high levels of confidence, our data shows—breathtakingly high. British women feel as confident as British men in their financial acumen, and twice as confident as American women. Women under the age of 40 are 2.6 times more confident than those age 40 and above; women with at least $1 million in assets are 32% more confident than women with less than a million. This is striking, because female investors in the UK are actually less financially savvy (in terms of the number of women in our sample who passed the basic financial literacy assessment) than they think they are, and certainly less savvy than their US counterparts (whose confidence, as we saw in the last chapter, is quite low).

Birgit Neu, co-chair of The Network of Networks for Gender, formerly with HSBC, says she's not at all surprised by lower levels of financial acumen, given the paucity of financial education offered to both men and women throughout their schooling. Compounding the lack of education, she says, is women's tendency to keep finance out of their conversation with other women. "Men talk to each other about their investments, but women won't even broach the topic with other women," she observes. "They keep their finances to themselves." Sofat says that her clients are financially savvy, but ask for a lot more information before making a decision—indicative, she says, of their deliberative approach. "Women like to have one hundred percent of the facts; men will act on eighty percent," she observes. However, she does see a greater "numbers phobia" among men and women in the UK than in her native India. "I think it's in the way math is taught," she muses. "I spent my primary school years in India and I have no fear of numbers. But my brother was educated in the UK and he's quite phobic."

Figure 5.6
I feel confident in my financial knowledge
(UK)

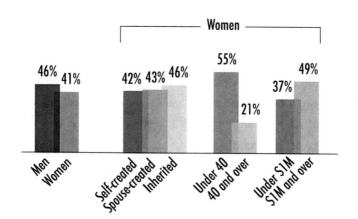

Literacy levels aside, women's high confidence translates into a notable absence of risk aversion. Our research shows UK women to be as embracing of risk as UK men, with less than a third describing themselves as risk-averse. And their assessment of risk tolerance aligns rather consistently with their actual tolerance, with the exception of inheritors, who are almost twice as likely to *perceive* themselves as risk-averse as they are to *be* risk-averse (23% versus 13%).

What accounts for this remarkable risk tolerance? Helena Morrissey, CEO of Newton Investments, points to British investors' predilection, historically speaking, for real estate. The proportion of household wealth tied up in property is significantly greater in the UK, she says, than for anywhere else in the developed world, in part because with so little property to go around, property values remain consistently high. Hence individuals invested largely in real estate have simply not experienced the volatility with their portfolio that investors with wealth allocated to the markets have suffered. "They're more accustomed to leveraging a small amount of equity in real estate into higher returns from rising real estate prices," Morrissey observes, "so they lack a heightened sense of vulnerability."

Figure 5.7
Perceived vs. actual risk appetite
(UK)

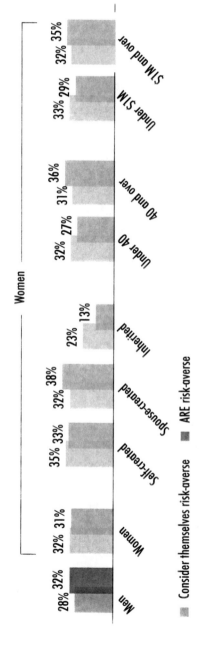

— Women —

| | Consider themselves risk-averse | | ARE risk-averse |

Men 28% 32%
Women 32% 31%
Self-treated 35% 33%
Spouse-treated 32% 38%
Inherited 23% 13%
Under 40 32% 27%
40 and over 31% 36%
Under $1M 33% 29%
$1M and over 32% 35%

* "Consider themselves risk-averse" is derived from responses to the question "Do you consider yourself..." with Likert scale responses spanning "Extremely" to "Not at all" risk-averse. "Are risk-averse" is based on the question "Which of these investment options would you like to own?" with responses ranging from "Very risky" to "Somewhat risky" to "Not at all risky." We denoted those who picked the least risky option as risk-averse.

Figure 5.8
What is the portfolio allocation of assets held in your name only?*
(Women)

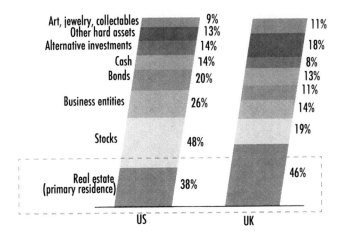

* Numbers in the chart do not add up to 100% because they are computed by first calculating the relevant
proportions at the individual level, and then averaging the proportions for each asset type.

Jamie Broderick of UBS says this data squares with his experience of female investors. "The female clients we deal with, by and large, are undifferentiated from male clients in terms of their financial confidence and risk aversion," he observes. Like men, they expect returns, and often they prefer the same products. Marketing efforts to target British women investors as distinct from men haven't borne fruit, he says. "Our experience has been, that a female entrepreneur wants to be talked to as an entrepreneur, not as a woman." Source of wealth is the real differentiator among women, he adds, as style preferences and goals differ for wealth creators, inheritors, and spouses.

ALTRUISM

The one area where wealth creators aren't at the leading edge of the female investor market is philanthropy. Inheritors drive investment in charitable enterprises, our research shows, in accordance with a long tradition of *noblesse oblige* and a habit of charitable giving that begins in secondary school. At venerable institutions like Eton, our interviewees told us, putting in community service time and raising money for local nonprofits is expected of all students, as philanthropy is a cherished school value.

Philanthropy is something Broderick and his team at UBS are increasingly focused on, as his newer-wealth clients recognize they need help strategizing their legacy. "People are more skeptical about giving all their wealth to their kids," he notes. "So there's a greater awareness of philanthropy among our clients." Helping Gen X and Boomer clients set up charitable foundations, he says, has turned out to be one key aspect of his business.

What's new, our industry specialists point out, is interest among the wealthy in a greater array of social-impact investing opportunities. Indeed, we find that 82% of British women want to invest in companies that promote social good and 84% want to invest in organizations whose goals align with their own. Broderick is building out his team's values-based offerings, as the definition of what constitutes a social enterprise has recently become less murky in the UK. "There's still more talk than uptake," he says, "but we're definitely seeing a shift toward socially aware investing." Morrissey, too, speaks to the trend and its impact on Newton's investment analysis. "Even in the absence of applying negative screening, there's an expectation the fund manager will take a proactively ethical approach," she says. "So we've embedded this in our mainstream analysis, evaluating companies on how responsibly they're managed and how sustainable their practices are."

Increasingly, Morrissey says, those intent on making socially-responsible investments are keen to see companies held to a higher diversity and gender-equality code. Both individuals and institutions are bringing this pressure to bear, scrutinizing not just the investment but also the advisory team for a better mix of women and minorities in management. The increased market demand for greater diversity in the UK mirrors the observations highlighted in Chapter 3, where senior women in the industry like Elaine are being more vocal about the value of diversity. Morrissey says that the finance directors of charitable foundations want to see, on Morrissey's team, more women, as the directors themselves are now women. Helping investors hold companies to account for their diversity is a change in corporate governance code that makes diversity and inclusion policies and metrics more transparent—including the number of women serving on the company's board.

Figure 5.9
Do you want to invest in any of the following causes?
(UK)

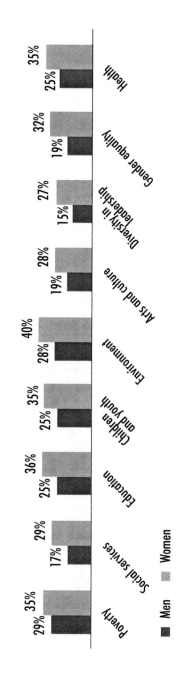

"It's early stages yet, but we're seeing an increased focus on board representation from investors," Morrissey notes. "We expect to see more of them engaging with management to discuss gender and other diversity issues." Her own Thirty Percent Club, an initiative to increase the number of women on boards, is also helping leverage change, as members will vote against a roster of annual election candidates if it lacks adequate representation of women.

WHAT BRITISH WOMEN WANT FROM WEALTH ADVISORY

Sofat describes the new wealth management paradigm as needing to address three interconnected priorities for women: financial return, personal return, and social return. To understand how women will allocate their resources, advisors must first understand "the big picture," or the larger vision women have for themselves as change agents, her experience indicates. Acquiring that understanding can be a time-consuming process, but in the end, she says, such an approach pays two-fold because women remain loyal and refer all their friends. "Women aren't looking for female advisors," she clarifies. "They're looking for someone they can trust."

We heard this over and over from women in our UK focus groups, many of whom, despite earning a living in finance, had little time to apply their know-how to their own finances. "My financial arrangements go right to the bottom of the pile," one investment banker in mergers and acquisitions told us. Her job remit was changing; she was about to be split between London and Hong Kong, and dreaded having to shop for the expertise that managing her newly complicated income scenario warranted. "I'd hand over my finances if I could find someone I could trust and who would help me align my larger life decisions with my financial goals and objectives," she said. "Frankly, I would trade returns for trust."

Other breadwinners echoed a desire to delegate not decision-making but worry and anxiety. One described lying awake at night fretting about "what ifs" in terms of her income being adequate to her children's educational needs and her retirement, in part because she didn't trust that her advisor fully understood her. "It's really about that person across the table not trying to sell to you but to ask you the right questions," she explains. "But often what you find is that when you go into a meeting they have off-the-shelf products lined up on beautiful stock paper. They don't ask you anything. They walk you through these brochures and they haven't bothered to learn a thing about you."

Men, too, Sofat hastens to clarify, don't want the conversation to be all about product. But either they worry less or they're not prepared to discuss their long-term vision, whereas women want a financial plan that makes possible their long-term goals and aren't prepared to discuss product until they're confident their advisor knows what they're trying to achieve with their money. They're prepared to be hands-on, she says, but need a framework, a financial plan that reconciles personal goals with professional aspirations, personal welfare with societal betterment.

"Women can seem emotional about their fears," she observes, "but they're very rational when it comes to decision making. The key, for advisors, is to help them marry their plans."

6

What Asian Women Want
(India, China, Hong Kong, and Singapore)

The face of wealth in Asia isn't what it was a generation ago. Today, it's increasingly young, worldly, supremely confident—and female.

China boasts the most self-made female entrepreneurs in the world.[35] Li Jing* is one of them. Like many of her generation—the first to avail themselves, in the late 1980s, of educational opportunities in the US— Li Jing burned with ambition to forge a life for herself very different from that of her parents. Born in Shanghai, she attended Calvin College in Michigan, and then won admission to Harvard Business School. That gilded MBA opened doors for her in Silicon Valley, where she gained invaluable experience as a product manager for Sun Microsystems. But after working as an electrical engineer and project manager for General Motors, Li Jing found herself yearning for her native China. Its economy was exploding; in particular, with over one billion mobile users, the mobile market beckoned with business opportunity. In 2000, she moved back to Shanghai and founded a mobile marketing service

* pseudonym used at interviewee's request

INVESTOR SNAPSHOT

(WOMEN WITH $1 MILLION OR MORE IN ASSETS HELD IN THEIR NAME)

AN UNTAPPED MARKET

51% don't have an advisor
77% with advisors feel misunderstood
76% are decision makers over household assets

"WEALTH MEANS TO ME..."

77% financial security
55% financial independence
53% funding my aspirations, driving my agenda
37% greater career latitude
32% a more luxurious lifestyle

DECISION-MAKING FACTORS

46% feel confident in their financial acumen
19% perceive themselves as risk-averse
25% are risk-averse

VALUES AGENDA

92% want to invest in organizations that promote social well-being

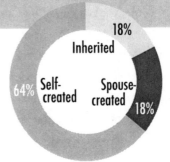

18%
Inherited

64% Self-created

Spouse-created 18%

company. Her firm, which allows corporate customers to identify and attract consumers through interactive mobile messaging, today represents one of the most efficient target marketing solutions and consulting services in China. In 2011, Tokyo-based MGI (Mitsui Global Investment) announced its investment in her firm, establishing Li Jing as one of China's rising corporate leaders.

Li Jing is in excellent company with a cadre of business- and tech-savvy women who are accustomed to making financial decisions that affect billions in corporate assets. These businesswomen are controlling and deploying significant personal assets, too. Married with no children, Li Jing is emblematic of the Gen X women at the leading edge of this trend. "I'm entirely focused on building my business," she says. "The mobile market moves incredibly fast, and even though we're no longer in our adolescence as a company, I can't afford to miss opportunities to ensure our continued growth."

Jing's focus is matched by that of Olivia Lum, the founder and CEO of Hyflux, a Singapore company providing governments all over the world with innovative products and systems to create potable water for more of their citizens. A chemist by training, Lum started out at Glaxo Pharmaceutical after completing school in Singapore. But when many of her peers opted to climb the corporate ladder, Lum liquidated her modest assets to seed a venture that would become the world's premier water-treatment company. "It was clear to me the world was going to run out of clean water," she says. "No one wanted to start a water business then, but I had this one passion. I wanted to save the world." In 2001, Hyflux became the first water treatment company to be listed on the Singapore Stock Exchange. Today, Lum is worth $305 million.[36]

This trend of female wealth creators with links to the West can be seen throughout the region. Pollyanna Chu is a Hong Kong native who immigrated to the US when she was 18, made a fortune in real estate with her husband, also an émigré, and then moved back to Hong Kong to cofound Kingston Securities, a securities trading, futures trading, corporate finance, and asset management firm where she is chief executive.

Women are on the rise in Central Asia, too. Namrata Suri, a marketing and advertising consultant, is one of them. She oversees business development for Olive Telecommunication in Gurgaon, India. Back in the 1980s, she began her career in local print media. In the mid-1990s, she founded the National Institute of Advertising, an industry group focused on educating and networking India's burgeoning communications professionals. Today, she's CEO of Interfirm, helping Western companies position their brands in India. As someone who out-earns most of the men in her family and social circle, Suri has achieved financial security. Now in her late 40s, her goals are around growing her business to establish her legacy.

FILLING THE PURSE—AND CONTROLLING IT

Jing, Lum, Chu, and Suri are emblematic of a rising tide of female wealth and confidence in Asia. They have emerged within the context of unprecedented national economic growth and high employment rates. Asia's boom over the past decade has accelerated the exponential growth of the female market. As one example: China's GDP growth in 2013 and 2014 totaled 7.7% and 7.4% respectively, outpacing that of most global emerging markets.[37] China has the highest rate of female employment in the world—64% of women work.[38] Economic liberalization and a robust stock market have catapulted many Chinese into sudden wealth. In 2013, *Forbes* magazine put the count of Chinese billionaires at 168, second only to the US.[39] Though the burgeoning opportunities for industry are still dominated by men, more women—especially those educated abroad—are starting businesses. They're also starting to be the beneficiaries of first-generation wealth created by their fathers.

The same is true in India. In a country where historically women held less than 10.9% of land[40] and controlled no assets, these portraits of power point to nothing short of a cultural revolution, one with profound implications for the wealth management industry. Twenty-four percent of Indian women work.[41] Thirty-nine percent have tertiary degrees.[42] And 86% of those holding professional roles, according to data CTI harvested in 2010, hunger for evermore lucrative and challenging assignments.[43] By their 30s professional women, Suri observes, hold bank accounts and real estate in their own name and have control, solely or jointly, of investable assets; by their 40s, they've inherited family wealth. The most significant wealth transfer, CTI's qualitative research suggests, is occurring even earlier: prominent family business owners are moving their 20-something daughters into power. One wealth advisor we interviewed in India told us that women who'd attended graduate and MBA schools in the US or Europe and then returned to India to run the family business represent the single greatest market opportunity for the industry. "They're not only managing a significant amount of family wealth, they're also now on the brink of a steep accumulation phase of their own personal wealth as the executive running the family business," he says. "It's a huge double play."

As a result of the economic boom in the region, women have newly become one of the greatest growth markets for the financial services industry. In particular the composition of the market, as we saw in Chapter 3, is strikingly tilted towards wealth creators, similar to the market dynamics we observed in the US and UK. Our research validates the experiences of Indian women like Suri: 59% of the women in our sample report that they're generating their wealth; only 20% derive it from their spouse, and 21% inherit it. Hong Kong offers especially fertile ground for women to grow their assets. Fully 68% of women in our Hong Kong sample—the highest percentage of any country, in line with mainland China (68%) and Singapore (67%)—say that they are the creators of their household wealth. Their wealth is substantial, and it is growing: 58% of women surveyed across the four countries, for example, expect their assets to increase.

Women don't merely fill the purse in Asia: they control it. The vast majority of women we surveyed across the four economies in Asia are financial decision makers in their households. As we showed in Chapter 1, 80% of Indian women are decision makers in their households, as are 87% of Chinese women. In Hong Kong, 71% of women report themselves to be decision makers over household assets; in Singapore, 59% of women in Singapore say they're decision makers. Compare these numbers to those in the US, where 44% of American women self-describe as decision makers. The respect attendant on women as a result of this power is one of the biggest cultural differences between the West and Asia, according to those we interviewed.

Figure 6.1
Decision makers over household assets

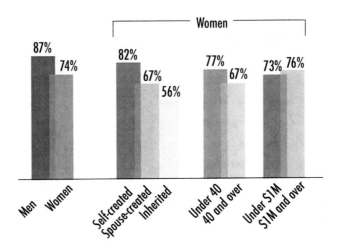

As spouses, the women surveyed in Singapore are less likely than women in the rest of Asia to claim decision-making power, but cultural recognition of women as men's equals means they nonetheless have their say over household assets. "If wealth is held jointly, men do give leeway to their spouse to make decisions" says Mabel Chua, group head of Southeast Asia and a managing director at Deutsche Bank's private wealth management. This joint decision-making is most prevalent for couples we frequently serve in the $1 million to $10 million net worth range, she says. "Women are absolutely seen as equal partners," affirms Judy Hsu, a wealth advisor at Standard Charted.

Gender parity means that Singapore women, whether single or married, are expected to be financially independent. "There is less emphasis here on the traditional gender expectations than in Malaysia or Indonesia," says Rajan Raju, a managing director at Deutsche Bank.

In Hong Kong, women also seem to benefit from a history of parity. "Female leadership is culturally accepted here," says Florence Kui, herself a leader as chief operating officer for Goldman Sachs private wealth management in Asia. "At the highest levels in government as well as in business, you'll find women." She adds, "Women may be more confident taking lead roles in Hong Kong because Chinese men are more comfortable with women being the key decision makers regarding money." These factors help explain why we found high numbers of women in the Asian countries reporting themselves to be decision makers over household assets.

And yet despite high levels of engagement among women in Asia, we still see tremendous market failure. Against a backdrop of massive wealth accumulation, Asia's richest aren't seeking wealth managers. Only seven percent of China's more than $4 trillion in investable assets are today under management, according to an Accenture Wealth and Asset Management Services study.[44] This represents a significant opportunity for wealth managers who understand the investment needs of Asian women.

MORE CONFIDENT INVESTORS

Women in Asia are more confident investors than their female counterparts in the US. They are remarkably confident about their financial know-how, though they're not commensurately literate—not by a long shot.

There are nuances to this picture worth noting. For example, women in India and China are more confident than women in Hong Kong and Singapore. Our research also uncovered that women under 40 in China, Hong Kong, and Singapore are interestingly more confident than those investors age 40 and over, while there is almost no divergence by age for women in India. Female creators in India, however, are significantly more confident than spouse creators or inheritors.

Figure 6.2
I feel confident about my financial knowledge

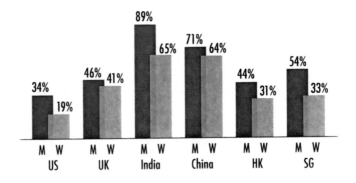

These nuances point to important cultural factors. As Subha Barry a consultant and formerly of Merrill Lynch noted (in Chapter 4), Western women often struggle with deeply engrained cultural mores that dictate that men, not women, take charge of major financial decisions; Asian women do not face the same pressures. The impact of this cultural difference shows up in the data. Indian women are among the most confident of all the female investors we surveyed, though not as confident as Indian men (65% versus 89%). They're not commensurately knowledgeable about finance, but we did not find a significant difference in financial literacy between men and women. Women wealth creators (as compared to spouses and inheritors) are the most confident—irrespective of generation and wealth level. Barry finds none of this surprising. "Even in rural India, women manage the households and pay the bills," she says. "Women's confidence comes from having handled money from an early age."

In China, women are both financially literate and extremely confident. Li Jing is a case in point. Her financial savvy and confidence is the result, she says, of both her Western education and her upbringing. "I never encountered gender bias," she states. An upside to the Communist legacy, she observes, is that women don't suffer the stigma and barriers in male-dominated industries that their Western counterparts suffer. China's longstanding (and recently revoked) one-child policy has ensured daughters enjoy the same opportunities as sons. Men as well as women, according to Kui of Goldman Sachs, bring daughters to wealth advisory meetings to educate them early.

The traditional view of women as subordinates hasn't been entirely purged, however. Dominique Boer, head of relationship management for Asia and Greater China at Standard Chartered, explains that geography, even more than generation, must be taken into account when parsing the power of the female investor. It may not be unusual to see in some parts of China, she says, "that women are key influencers but take a back seat to men in public." Whereas in Shanghai, "it's not uncommon to see women in control of all financial decisions, as women there have a long history as 'money makers' controlling gold and spice trades."

In consideration of the differences that surfaced between women in China and India as compared to American women, the maturity of the wealth management industry in Asia may be a factor. Because the wealth management industry in Asia is still emerging, its financial services products are somewhat less complex than those in the American markets. The incredible complexity of US financial instruments may account for the cautiousness of American women investors as compared to their Asian counterparts.

RISK: A MIXED BAG

Confident investors do seem to be more comfortable with risk. In China, for example, we found almost no gender gap in terms of actual risk appetite among investors who responded to our survey. India was the anomaly: confidence doesn't necessarily translate into an appetite for risk. The majority (52%) of Indian women assess themselves as risk-averse. But that assessment turns out to be largely perception: only 22% actually preferred investments that are low risk. Women in India and China are more risk tolerant than women we sampled in the US and UK (78% of Indian and Chinese women selected a moderate or aggressive portfolio, versus 64% in the US and 69% in the UK).

While they do not self-assess as particularly risk averse, it is notable that women in Singapore were the most likely to prefer low risk investments as compared to other women in Asia (62% of women surveyed in Singapore selected a moderate or aggressive portfolio). On the whole, female wealth creators, spouses, and inheritors in China and Hong Kong, our global data shows, self-assess as highly confident investors with greater appetite for risk—a very different portrait from that sketched by women in the US, the UK, and India.

Figure 6.3
Perceived risk vs. actual risk appetite

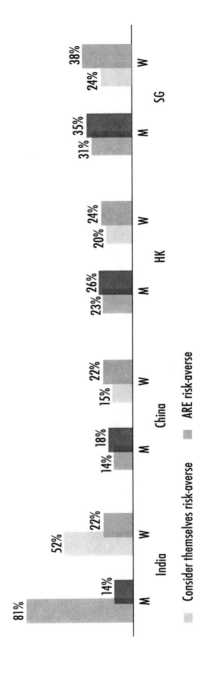

NEW WEALTH, NEW WANTS

What do women in Asia want from wealth? As in the US and UK, women in our sample want from their wealth financial security and independence.

But we see interesting contrasts within Asia. Whereas there are gender differences in India and Hong Kong, women and men in China and Singapore want virtually the same things from their wealth: financial security and the ability to fund aspirations and drive agendas. Certainly this is the focus of Hong Kong entrepreneur Pollyanna Chu. Her legacy, not her affluent lifestyle, is what she wants her wealth to secure.[45]

Wealth means very different things for men and women in India. Like women in the US and UK, Indian women place much greater emphasis on funding their aspirations and career latitude. They are much more likely than men to see wealth as Namrata Suri does: as a means to fund their aspirations and drive their agendas (46% of Indian women see it this way, as compared to a mere 26% of men). Thirty-nine percent of Indian women want wealth to offer them career latitude, as opposed to 21% of men—making them 86% more likely to equate wealth with career growth. The emphasis on wealth as a means to fund aspirations is particularly true for wealth inheritors, 67% of whom value wealth for the opportunity it affords to drive their own agendas.

WHAT DOES HAVING WEALTH MEAN TO YOU?
(INDIA, CHINA, HONG KONG, AND SINGAPORE)

Figure 6.4
What does having wealth mean to you? (India)
(By gender)

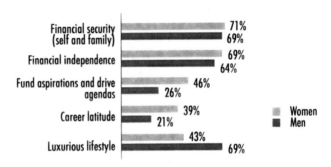

Figure 6.5
What does having wealth mean to you? (China)
(By gender)

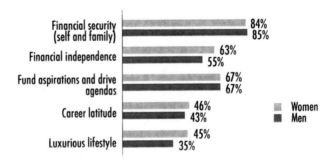

Figure 6.6
What does having wealth mean to you? (Hong Kong)
(By gender)

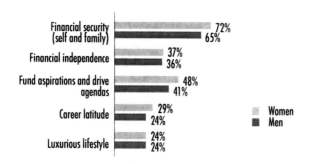

	Women	Men
Financial security (self and family)	72%	65%
Financial independence	37%	36%
Fund aspirations and drive agendas	48%	41%
Career latitude	29%	24%
Luxurious lifestyle	24%	24%

Figure 6.7
What does having wealth mean to you? (Singapore)
(By gender)

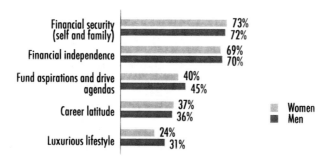

	Women	Men
Financial security (self and family)	73%	72%
Financial independence	69%	70%
Fund aspirations and drive agendas	40%	45%
Career latitude	37%	36%
Luxurious lifestyle	24%	31%

The most stunning gender difference we uncovered concerns how Indians value a luxurious lifestyle; a robust majority (69%) of men equate wealth with luxury, as compared to 43% of women. Nowhere else in our global sample is luxury accorded so much emphasis. While a luxurious lifestyle is less important for both men and women in China than in the rest of Asia, women desire it more than men, especially those who have inherited wealth. The Chinese women we surveyed are 29% more likely than men to define wealth this way. Chinese customers are the world's biggest luxury buyers by nationality, and women make up three fifths of China's $39 billion luxury market.[46] Our data shows inheritors to be the most likely to prioritize a luxurious lifestyle.

HEIGHTENED SOCIAL CONSCIENCE

Yet it would be a mistake to interpret this focus on the finer things as a disinterest in philanthropy or social impact. CTI research shows that both men and women in China as well as in the other three countries in Asia want to have societal impact, and in a big way.

Nearly the entire China survey cohort (98%) says that "making a positive impact on society" is important as is "investing in organizations that invest in social good" (97%). Chinese women say they want to donate and invest in causes important to them, and they do. Fully 70% of female investors in China say they want to invest in education and 69% say they want to invest in gender equality—and a similar proportion has indeed made these investments. These findings surprised advisors whom we interviewed, as it is commonly assumed that the Chinese are tight-fisted when it comes to charity. "In my experience, most women in Asia tend to plan for their children first, not charity," says Deutsche Bank advisor Sheau-Yuen Tan.

While the wealthy in Hong Kong still indulge in luxurious-lifestyle products, says Marina Lui, a managing director who heads up ultra-high-net-worth wealth management for UBS in China and Taiwan, there's "big awareness" around social-impact investing and philanthropy there—the strongest interest of any Asian market. "My clients like to give and invest on their own terms, though," she observes. "For mainland Chinese clients, giving is more ad hoc, less structured. Only some of them are looking to set up foundations to handle their philanthropic matters." High-net-worth women in Hong Kong, we find, are giving robustly to education, health, and the environment, whether as wealth generators, spouses, or inheritors.

In Singapore, philanthropy is as new as the wealth behind it. While the desire among both men and women to address social ills is quite high, with 89% of men and 92% of women keen to invest in organizations that invest in social enterprise, a much smaller percentage is executing on this desire. Singapore would seem generous only in comparison to our cohort in Hong Kong—and far less generous than China and India.

What distinguishes Asia from the US and UK in terms of philanthropy is the gender gap; in the West, more women than men are keen to invest in the social good, whereas in Asia, men are just as intent as women to improve education, eradicate poverty, and clean up the environment.

LEADING THE WAY ON DIVERSITY

Financial advisory services tend to reflect the Asian market: they are new, young, and on the ascendancy. Wealth management teams feature higher proportions of female advisors than their counterparts in the US and UK, suggesting they're steps ahead in developing advisor teams with gender smarts.

Look at wealth management in India, which according to advisors at Standard Chartered is only about 20 years old. Having come of age with this generation of professional women and billionaire heiresses, it shows every sign of being attuned to them. Advisory teams feature women: the proportion of female relationship managers to male, according to teams we interviewed, is about 60:40, and while the investment advisor is more often male (80:20), the branch manager is quite often a woman. Investment products, too, are evermore tailored to the needs of female business owners, thanks in part to a government mandate to expand offerings to this sector. "Women are perceived as leading and sustaining the economic boom," we heard in focus groups we conducted in Mumbai.

Thanks to the gender-equality legacy of Communism in China, women are exceedingly well represented in financial services there, too. Women outnumber men on advisory teams three to two, according to a recent Korn/Ferry report,[47] and can be found at the highest rungs of corporate governance, not only in finance but across industry sectors and in government. In these measures of economic empowerment and representation in leadership, it is tempting to infer a robust correlation.

In Southeast Asia, about three-quarters of wealth advisors in Singapore are women, our interviewees tell us—a function of Singapore's two-child policy, which ensures women enjoy the same opportunities as men. Even at senior levels, women are far more prevalent than in Western offices of the same bank: at Deutsche Bank's Asia operations, fully 25% of top managers are women. "It's simply good business to ensure gender parity in our ranks throughout the organization, particularly on the front lines," one of our senior-level interviewees explained. "Wealth management is a relationship business, where soft skills matter, and there is a general market perception that women manage the role better—from client communication and honesty to transparency and efficiency."

AN EMPHASIS ON SERVICE

Courting the female market in Asia, wealth advisors from every bank stressed, does not necessitate forming teams of women, although as we just saw, throughout Asia, women advisors and relationship managers do significantly outnumber men (and many of those women are in senior management positions, according to Marina Lui of UBS). Rather, it's what women bring to their teams that warrants emphasis. As a Standard Chartered relationship manager notes, "If you take care of the little things, women will trust you and want to listen to your ideas." That can mean helping women not just to fund their child's education, but also to find the child an appropriate school to attend, according to Dominique Boer, head of relationship management for Asian and Greater China at Standard Chartered. "Female client satisfaction is driven by their client service experience and value-add services," Boer adds. "Performance is important, of course. But they're looking for advisors who adopt, as they do, a holistic approach to wealth planning." Advisors eager to capitalize on the female wealth market opportunity in Asia would do well to adopt such a service-oriented approach. As we'll see in the next chapter, for advisors in every market, service is the key to harnessing the power of the purse.

PART THREE
CLOSING THE GAP

7

Becoming Gender Smart: Embedding Acquired Diversity Inside and Out

Our six-country dataset makes clear just how much wealth goes untapped when advisors and wealth management firms fail to engage female investors as they differ by market segment. Our findings underscore the imperative of recognizing women as wealth creators and decision makers, and not just spouses and inheritors; of perceiving how women differ from each other, depending on their age, culture, and level of assets; and of understanding that women wish to invest their assets in ways that advance their personal, professional, and social-betterment agenda as well as their financial independence and security.

So what will it take to unlock all this potential—and take the money off the table?

CTI's groundbreaking research on innovation, diversity, and market growth points to the answer for the industry: advisors on the front line as well as leaders within advisory firms need both to embody and embrace gender diversity. Simply put, that means more advisors and leaders either need to *be* women, or be leaders with "gender smarts," leaders who have *acquired* an appreciation for the value proposition women hold (as it may differ from men's) and the ways in which women process information, arrive at decisions, and take action. Our 2013 research shows that at publicly held companies where leadership has both inherent and acquired diversity—where leaders both embody and embrace difference—employees are 70% more likely to report that the company captured a new market in the last year, and 45% more likely to report that it grew market share, than employees at companies lacking this 2D Diversity®.[48]

Figure 7.1
The Diversity Dividend

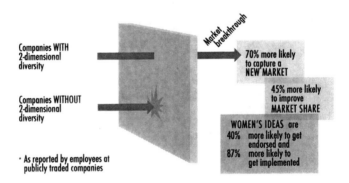

Companies WITH 2-dimensional diversity

Companies WITHOUT 2-dimensional diversity

• As reported by employees at publicly traded companies

Market breakthrough

70% more likely to capture a NEW MARKET

45% more likely to improve MARKET SHARE

WOMEN'S IDEAS are
40% more likely to get endorsed and
87% more likely to get implemented

Why should 2D Diversity® make such a difference in market growth? Certainly it makes sense that customer-facing employees who look like their customers might engage with them more easily; and similarly, that teams tasked with innovating for a certain consumer might do better at identifying that consumer's unmet needs if someone on the team *was* that customer. Our 2013 findings bear that out: teams with at least one member who represents the end-user are upwards of 158% more likely than teams without that representation to understand that end-user. But that superior understanding of the end-user only translates into innovation, we find, when that team member feels welcome and included and free to share her ideas or opinions. If she doesn't feel included, if she feels her ideas won't be heard or recognized, she won't speak up. And then her ability to apply her unique insight to identify unmet needs and propose solutions is lost to the team. The team doesn't benefit from her inherently different perspective.

In other words, to capture a new market segment it's not enough to have team members who look like that market. Teams need leaders who can unlock valuable end-user insights by making everyone on the team feel included enough to contribute, particularly those who represent the end-user. We identified in our 2013 study *Innovation, Diversity, and Market Growth* six behaviors that prove to be highly correlated with a "speak-up culture," or an environment in which all members feel welcome to contribute their ideas. Making sure the quietest voice in the room gets heard, taking feedback and acting on it, sharing constructive feedback, sharing credit for team success, empowering team members with decision making, and making it safe for members to propose risky ideas turn out to unlock the insights that lead to innovation that culminates in market growth.

But here's what's really interesting: these six inclusive leader behaviors are highly correlated with acquired diversity traits such as gender smarts. Gender-smart men, that is, are more likely to be inclusive leaders. They're more likely to behave in ways that make women feel included and inclined to express their ideas and opinions. With women contributing to the number of ideas that fill the innovation pipeline, and leaders supporting ideas that come from women, more innovation is likely to emerge that will appeal to women.

And therein lies the power of 2D Diversity®. Companies that succeed in fostering a speak-up culture through inclusive leadership measurably outperform the competition, our data affirms.

The problem for financial services and wealth management firms is that most are helmed by men who lack gender smarts. Only 32% of professionals we sampled who work in financial services report that leadership at their firm manifests 2D Diversity®.[49] The majority work at firms where women may be well represented in the lower rungs and to a lesser extent on the front lines, but aren't well represented in leadership. They're part of an organization where those who perceive or empathize with the unmet needs and wants of female investors struggle to find an audience that is both receptive and empowered to act on their insights or ideas. Indeed, more than half of all professionals we surveyed (56%) in our 2013 study say leaders at their firm fail to see value in ideas that they personally don't see a need for. This lack of gender smarts translates into a chokehold that disproportionately suppresses innovation from women. At companies lacking 2D Diversity* in leadership, we find, women's ideas are less likely to get traction: straight white men are 28% more likely to win endorsement for their ideas than are women.

INFRASTRUCTURE CHALLENGES

Most financial service firms suffer from what might be termed the homogeneity tax: they're not hearing from, or not acting on, ideas with the power to unlock the female investor market globally. The issue is twofold: firms in the US and UK are struggling to attract a larger cadre of women into the business. Asian firms have inherent diversity in the ranks—women are, after all, relationship managers, advisors, and private bankers in relatively equal numbers. But absent women and gender-smart men at the top of the house who create the inclusive environment in which market-worthy ideas get elicited and endorsed, these firms aren't likely to bring to market the kind of products and the kind of service that would engage women as investors and decision makers. Nor are they likely to attract talented women in the US and UK to the industry.

The physically distributed nature of the wealth management industry, particularly in the US, can make diversifying its talent an even greater challenge.

Advisors are generally located in communities proximate to their target client base. The smaller, local-office (versus centralized-headquarters) model makes it incrementally tougher for firms to build a critical mass of female advisors in each location, and to create a feeling of connection between women in those offices and successful female advisors or managers in other locations.

"Promising female talent can sometimes lack more senior female role models that are local, particularly in smaller offices," points out Megan Taylor, chief operating officer of private wealth management at Goldman Sachs. "The lack of accessible role models can place women at greater risk during inflection points in their professional careers or personal lives." She credits Goldman's proactive efforts around networking and sponsorship programs with the firm's success in retaining younger female advisors, particularly during the years when they are building their business and potentially also establishing families. "Support and advice from someone who has successfully navigated the same situation can make a significant difference," she adds. "It helps to both validate a person's feelings, while also providing the confidence to work through the situation."

Both male and female advisors face several important and potentially difficult-to-navigate career inflection points: establishing a book of business, choosing a partner or team, negotiating the breakdown of team economics, and positioning for a promotion, to name just a few. Each of these inflection points results in some level of natural attrition, which is generally consistent across genders. The most notable difference between male and female attrition levels relates to managing time off for family commitments, such as the addition of a child or needing to provide eldercare. Our research shows that a key factor in a female advisor's ability to successfully navigate these situations on a professional level is a constructive, team-based coverage model. "When a woman takes maternity or family leave, it is important that she is supported by a team that continues to help provide service and advice to her clients, otherwise the erosion of her client base can impact the prospects of a successful return," observes Nicole Pullen Ross, who heads up private wealth management for Goldman Sachs's mid-Atlantic region and is a former advisor herself.

The industry's entrepreneurial structure, one of the aspects which makes wealth management so attractive to female talent, can also ironically create barriers to developing the type of leadership profile and culture our research identifies as crucial. "Both men and women are attracted to the objective measures of success and the flexible, self-directed nature of the advisor role," notes Taylor. "However, the entrepreneurial and physically distributed business model can make it more difficult for managers to identify and cultivate the non-commercial-oriented talents of advisors." This situation can result in less visibility and sponsorship for advisors of either gender, when compared to other financial services roles. Sponsorship can be particularly challenging for women, who, according to Shona Baijal, a desk head in UBS's wealth management division in the UK, simply don't break through to upper management without it (she credits her own sponsor for keeping her on the road to management). When women are absent in upper management, prospective female clients (as we learned in Chapter 3) consider investing their assets elsewhere. "We have only one woman on the management committee, and she's head of HR," commented one Chicago-based investment advisor. "With so few women at the top, it's increasingly more difficult to attract and engage high-net-worth women."

The industry's historically product-centric business model has acted as a deterrent to diversity as well. Commission-based models have created incentives for advisors to sell complex products rather than big-picture solutions, short-term gains rather than holistic strategies. While men may have accepted a transaction-orientated approach, with women, explains a former wealth-management executive, it foments insecurity about their financial savvy. "Products are currently packaged for the advisor, not the client, to understand," she explains. "They're not user friendly; their descriptions are full of jargon, which tends to erode women's confidence and heighten their sensitivity to risk." What women want from advisors, as we shall explore in the next chapter at length, is an experience-based relationship, not a product-based one. Women want to feel understood as a person, and have their values reflected in their investments; women want to be educated, and feel they can ask questions and air their concerns. As product and performance increasingly become a commodity, the differentiator for clients—women certainly, but increasingly men as well—is holistic advice. Many female advisors we interviewed voiced a strong preference for a fiduciary model. Expanding the base of female advisors would help accelerate the industry's shift to this client-centered approach, and yet absent this approach, the industry will likely continue to struggle to engage women. Male advisors will continue to pitch products. And the industry will continue to suffer the homogeneity tax.

ACQUIRED DIVERSITY

The solution to this catch-22 is for leaders in wealth management firms to adopt inclusive behaviors, and for advisors to adopt behaviors that engage women and win their trust and loyalty. Our global survey clarifies which inclusive advisor behaviors are likeliest to drive trust, satisfaction and loyalty. Certainly good communication and efficiency have long been recognized as critical in winning over prospective female clients, but four other behaviors emerge from our research that speak to women's hunger for more education, transparency, and respectful engagement. These behaviors can absolutely be taught: in the next chapter, we're going to make clear what they are, how they manifest, and how they can be deployed tactically.

Figure 7.2
Earning the trust of female investors
(Behaviors that drive trust, satisfaction, and loyalty)

But from our interviews, it's clear that some leaders are indeed well along in their practice of inclusivity because at some point in their career, some impasse demanded that they *acquire* an appreciation for difference. Indeed, we see the correlation that our innovation research affirms between acquired diversity and inclusive leadership: that men who come to appreciate what people unlike themselves bring to the table are more likely than men without that appreciation to behave in ways that make those people feel welcome, free to contribute their ideas and opinions, and heard and recognized. An appreciation for "the other" can be acquired—and can in turn inspire the inclusive behaviors that create a speak-up culture (or safe space for others to open up).

Ken Coleman, co-managing partner at Fairport Asset Management with Heather Ettinger, learned the value of inclusive leadership during his first job, working in labor relations for a manufacturing plant. On the first day, his boss took him aside to share some pointers. "Here's the key, Coleman," the older man told him. "You've got to hate people." Determined to "get to yes" in some other way, Coleman opted for greater transparency. He'd first focus on understanding what was important to them as a way of opening the negotiation. "I know there are some difficult relationships between labor and management. I'm coming in with my eyes wide open and not trying to game you, so maybe we can have a reasonable relationship. Instead of 'one of us is going to win and one of us is going to lose,' let's figure out how we can reach a good outcome for both of us. If we can come up with a means to achieve that, then we have an opportunity to really work together." By establishing a forum for honest dialogue, Coleman says, and being willing to listen, he was able to build trust—the linchpin to real progress in any situation. "If I was going to get anything done," he reflects, "I had to be sincere."

Jamie Broderick, head of UBS's wealth management division in the UK, honed his inclusive skill set at home in an effort to better connect with his kids. When they were very young, he picked up Adele Faber's parenting manual, *How to Talk So Kids Will Listen & Listen So Kids Will Talk*. "It changed my life," he says. "They opened up." The benefits of creating a speak-up culture became even clearer, he says, when he tried the same principles on his wife. Broderick shared his epiphany with his colleagues, and put its precepts into practice at work. "That's what good client behavior is all about," he observes. "Slow down, pay attention, do more listening than talking, pause long enough to read the other person, and let them know they're being paid attention to." He adds, "You get a lot of mileage from people if you're able to acknowledge their views and contributions."

For Tom Huvane, senior vice president of wealth management with Huvane Wealth Management Group at UBS Financial Services Inc., and his teammates Brendan Murphy, senior wealth strategy associate, and Betsy Rivera, client service associate, the lightbulb moment was more of a blunt calculation. Women make up over 50% of the US population; from a demographic standpoint it made sense, he realized, to make his business more female-friendly. "Looking three to five years out, I saw women—particularly single, professional women—as a great referral source and a big growth opportunity," he says. "We weren't exactly ignoring women, but I realized we could do a better job of engaging them." So rather methodically, Huvane set out to understand the female investor market. He talked to friends in different industries with experience selling to women. He talked to authors who'd written books about the female market. He also talked to women themselves: with the help of his managing director Mara

Glassel (a woman), he hosted a series of focus groups with women over breakfast, lunch, and dinner. "We did not pitch UBS," he explains. "We asked the women who attended what they wanted from an advisory practice, and what would make them join one." He learned from these encounters that, more so than men, women want to be educated. "They don't need to know everything down to the last line," he explains. "But they need to feel that they understand their investments so they can make a decision they're comfortable with. You have to understand that as an advisor and be patient. If advisors were to execute on that one word, it would make a huge difference in women's loyalty."

Wisdom worth sharing—and in Chapter 8, we'll share even more of it.

8

Winning Women's Business:
A Road Map for Advisors

Anna Sofat remembers well how the evening call began: "If I need money to buy a second home, where could I get it—*and how quickly?*"

Sofat, founder and CEO of Addidi, a boutique financial services firm in London, also remembers what went through her mind at the time: given the rocky year her client Helen had just had in terms of revenues, buying a holiday property was a bit more edgy, putting some financial security at risk.

But hearing the exhaustion in Helen's voice, Sofat found herself assuring her that they would find a way to buy that second home. "I understood where she was coming from," Sofat says. "I understood she really needed to do this, and that she needed a project and a place to get away, and that returning to the same environment when she went on holiday wasn't going to be enough."

So Sofat liquidated some of Helen's assets to gather the capital necessary, and Helen purchased the getaway of her dreams. "She's more illiquid now but her property assets should be fine over time. I knew it was something she needed," Sofat explains. With less of Helen's assets under management, Addidi lost out on some fees. But Sofat says that's a small price to pay. "I'd rather have her as a client than tell her, 'That's not right for you' which would have been the proper thing to do. I did not want to put money before her need and risk our longer-term relationship" she observes.

Sofat's long-term approach to client satisfaction has made Addidi the boutique of choice among high-net-worth women. Many of her clients, female entrepreneurs and inheritors, have defected from "the big boys" in search of her empathetic, personal relationship style—Helen among them. Wealth management firms profess to want to get to know their high-net-worth clients, says Sofat, but only so far as is necessary to sell them on a specific product. Sofat works more inductively. "When I get to know a client, I don't have preconceived ideas or judgments about what's right and wrong," she says. She asks questions about a new client's lifestyle, priorities, preferences, goals, personality, and values. She takes the time to understand her client's appetite for risk, her knowledge about different financial topics; she will schedule more in-depth meetings on topics that are unfamiliar to the client. Regular check-ins keeps her abreast of her clients' shifting financial and personal priorities.

Such a hands-on approach is time consuming, Sofat concedes—but less time consuming, in the long run, than looking for new clients. "When things are choppy or there's financial uncertainty, most of our clients know where they're heading—and so do we," she says. "That's how we build their trust, and earn their loyalty."

To build a business of female clients, it isn't necessary to actually *be* female. That's what Tom Huvane, senior vice president of wealth management with Huvane Wealth Management Group at UBS Financial Services Inc., learned when he staged a series of breakfast focus groups with female investors in the greater New York area. "Women aren't necessarily looking to work with female advisors," he says. "What they want is a more engaging presentation. Most women learn through stories they can relate to, not from spreadsheets or PowerPoint presentations. And they're much more focused on the goals they're trying to achieve, not the products that may help them get there."

Huvane and his teammates Brendan Murphy, senior wealth strategy associate, and Betsy Rivera, client service associate, have changed their style accordingly. "We don't say, 'Hey, look at our results,' or 'We were written up here,' because women don't care if the market is up twelve percent and you're up only eleven," he observes. "They want to know if they have enough money to retire, to put their kids through college, to give their daughters a nice wedding." He's learned to ask women to walk them through their current plan to better understand what their goals are for themselves and their families. "It may take longer, but in the long run I do a better job if I understand how the family works," he says. "I don't just talk about investments, I discuss the kids, the parents, the extended family."

When he proposes investment strategies and products, Huvane again encourages female clients to ask any questions that arise—and answers them patiently. "Often male advisors get frustrated when women ask them lots of questions, but it's important to know that this is how they process information and make decisions," Huvane says. "Most of my female clients just want to fully understand what they are buying."

This dialogue and collaborative decision-making process will last quite some time, but Huvane says his patience pays off. He's learned that the line "Let me think about it" means something different from a female client than it does from a male client. "While some advisors may not take her seriously when they hear that, it is a huge part of her decision-making process. She gathers input from her friends, family, and colleagues, and spends time thinking and asking questions about the solutions you've proposed. It's critical to support her through that process, because only then is she ready to decide to move forward," says Huvane. "Once she does, her loyalty is very high. Women can be a great source of referrals, but you've got to make them comfortable in order to win their trust." Huvane's gender smarts are paying off, in a big way—90% of his new accounts come from referrals and nearly 90% of those referrals come from existing women clients.

For Nadia Allaudin, senior vice president of wealth management at Merrill Lynch, effective communication is the sine qua non of a successful advisory. That's because 75% of the wealth she and her partner manage (over $500 million) is controlled by women. "Women want and need communication," she says. "If advisors can't provide that, that's what turns women away or makes them feel disconnected."

It's a precept she and her partner have jointly committed to work on to ensure female clients received equal attention. Her partner became self-aware of his tendency to defer to the husbands during meetings with couples—even when it was the wife who was making all the money. Allaudin and her partner also talked about not overloading on financial lingo. "We risk losing people if we talk about our covered call strategy and the income it generates," Allaudin and her partner discovered together. "They don't know what we're talking about, and it intimidates them."

What Allaudin observes is that good communication is about asking questions—questions that cannot be answered by 'yes' or 'no' but rather, elicit thoughts and feelings. Throughout a client meeting, Allaudin takes pains to interrupt herself to ask, "Did you understand that? Would you like us to review that?" And most importantly: "How do you feel?"

That one question has secured her the trust and loyalty of her clientele. Allaudin met with a woman recently who admitted, "I don't know how to hire an advisor." Because of her net worth, many advisors had approached her, but she hadn't met anyone who'd engaged her or with whom she felt a connection. So rather than talk about private equity or 529 planning, Allaudin opened their meeting with, "Instead of me telling you what we do, tell me about how you feel about money. Tell me your feelings, your fears, and what you want to do with your wealth." The woman opened up, and Allaudin became her advisor. "Everyone has a story," she notes. "If you can give people a platform to share it that feels comfortable and safe, that's when you can unravel their needs and give great advice. They're not looking for just the S&P returns; it's so much more complex than that."

The mistake too many advisors commit, she explains, is to focus on the portfolio. As a team, Allaudin and her partner realized they had to address their client's deepest and most meaningful financial goals. "Sometimes the client's big concern is long-term care planning, insurance, education cost, or liability management," she says. "We learned that returns for their portfolio weren't necessarily our clients only financial concern."

So rather than simply focus on what her clients' returns needs to be, Allaudin spends most of her face-to-face meetings or phone calls understanding their life priorities and reviewing how well their financial goals align with them. "It's not just financial," she says. "You have to have a holistic point of view."

CRACKING THE CODE

Working with female clients doesn't have to be a mystery. As Anna Sofat demonstrates, gaining a deep understanding of women—what they value, what they worry about, what motivates them and inspires them— is what engenders trust, as women seek to have their priorities validated by their investment strategy. As Tom Huvane makes clear, what attracts and keeps women as clients is creating a safe space for asking questions and arriving at decisions. And as Nadia Allaudin points out, women respect integrity, transparency, and a willingness to have tough conversations.

Yet our research shows Huvane, Allaudin, and Sofat to be far from typical. Advisors are neither wielding the emotional intelligence nor taking pains to listen to female clients, resulting in the dramatic market failure we portrayed in Chapter 2: 53% of women surveyed across the six markets lack a financial advisor. Even women who have an advisor feel misunderstood. Trust is absent.

What does it take to build it?

In our global survey, we identified six behaviors that correlate most highly with women's trust, satisfaction, and loyalty. In aggregate, they comprise what we term "gender smarts." Advisors whom female clients trust, we find, are advisors who communicate well, create a safe space for clients, understand their clients, educate them, help them align their investment and life goals, and efficiently manage the client relationship.

Figure 8.1
Investors who are satisfied when their advisor...* (Women)

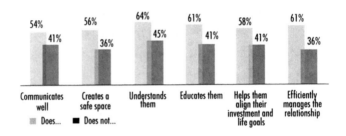

*Satisfaction = satisfied, trusting, and loyal

These behaviors are strikingly linked to women's unique value proposition as investors, and to the factors that guide their decision-making. With increasingly fast-paced lives, often with growing responsibilities at home *and* at work, women are starved for time. As a result, efficiency ranks among the most impactful of the six behaviors: advisors who are sensitive to women's constraints and readily manage details to conserve clients' time are 69% more likely to forge an enduring and satisfactory relationship than those who aren't efficient. Good communication, predictably, also rises to the top of the list of gender-smart behaviors. Advisors who communicate well are 32% more likely to earn female clients' trust, loyalty, and satisfaction.

Advisors who create a "safe space" for clients are 56% more likely to earn a woman's trust than advisors who don't create a safe space. Empathetic understanding is also key: an advisor who takes pains to understand a client's perspective, listen to her ideas, and learn about her family situation, values, and goals is 42% more likely to earn her trust and loyalty. Women want a relationship where they're encouraged to ask questions and can expect straightforward answers. And, it is critical to educate clients about risk and return of different investment options (advisors who educate their clients are 49% more likely to forge trust). Finally, helping clients align life and investment goals provides a 41% bump in advisors' likelihood to earn client trust.

What do these look like in practice? From our focus groups, interviews, and client engagements, we've harvested a cornucopia of tactics.

COMMUNICATE WELL

Brand yourself as a communicator. Eager to show women that he could engage on their terms, Huvane invited author Lee Woodruff, wife of journalist Bob Woodruff, to let him interview her in a public "Actors Studio"-like conversation over lunch with a group of successful professional women in New York. His questions elicited heartfelt answers from Woodruff, and he was able to demonstrate his ability to connect with women to the audience that gathered for the event. "This was way out of my comfort zone," he admits. "But women saw us together, and loved it."

Be authentic. "Many financial advisors—male and female—are far too scripted," one high-net-worth entrepreneur told us. "Their discussions seem guided by what they are told will sell a product or charge a fee. They forget to listen to what I actually want." Another said, "The first time I met our plan advisor, it was clear he was only asking me questions out of obligation, and didn't care about my concerns or expressed goals. It was incredibly frustrating." Clearly, a lack of authenticity is an easy way to alienate a female client.

Listen actively. Build trust by repeating back what you hear your client saying, as in: "Based on what I heard, I think you mean…did I hear you correctly?"

Be patient. Ensure you give your client enough time to digest and respond. After seeing many prospective clients simply nod, leave, and never return to his office after an initial meeting, a Seattle advisor realized that in an effort to "wow" his prospects he'd sucked up all the airtime. He now practices a 3:1 rule: for every one minute he speaks, he gives the client at least three minutes to respond.

Communicate on her terms. Find out how, and with what frequency, your client prefers to be contacted. An investor we interviewed in Chicago related this cautionary tale: "I asked my advisor to summarize her thoughts via email, because I just don't have time for a call. But she kept trying to set up these telephone calls with me. Eventually, I moved on to someone who could move at my pace." Flexibility on mode and frequency of communication can go a long way with clients.

CREATE A SAFE SPACE

Signal respect. Too often advisors ignore women in meetings with married couples, as they assume she is the least knowledgeable in the room—or the least interested. "In my experience, whenever I was in one of these meetings, there was no real attempt to involve me in conversation," says one female investor in London. "I certainly wasn't treated like a decision maker, let alone a wealth creator." By acknowledging her as a key decision maker at the outset of a meeting, an advisor can immediately set a tone of mutual respect with a female client.

Be vulnerable. Stories—not bullet points or performance metrics—establish meaningful dialogue with clients. Chris Dodd, a senior account executive at Fidelity, always shares a personal story to break the ice with new clients. "Women appreciate that someone across the table is willing to open up," he says.

Make your office feel like a refuge, not an exam room. Ameriprise Private Wealth Advisor Geri Eisenman Pell consciously decorated her office to project calm—from the Zen fountain, to the comfortable couches, to the statue of the meditating frog. "Stress and investment management don't have to go hand-in-hand," she says. Creating this calming environment has particularly paid off with her female clients, the majority of whom are single, widowed, or divorced, and are sole financial decision makers. "They call me their financial therapist," Pell says.

Comfortable couches work for Pell, but "safe" needn't be interpreted so literally. Some advisors create safe space by developing a respectful, clear tone with clients.

Save the jargon, use clear language. While both men and women told us they have trouble understanding jargon, women are more likely to feel their advisors are talking above their heads by employing jargon. Instead of rolling out complicated terms and acronyms, explain concepts and assume no foreknowledge of terminology. "My advisor needs to meet me where I am," says a female investor in Boston. "Too many times they try to impress me with *their* financial understanding instead of trying to work with mine."

Elicit questions. Keep pausing to ask if a client has questions. Wait a few seconds before resuming. As we saw in Chapter 3, one outcome of women's lack of financial confidence is a hesitancy to ask questions. Yet she needs to ask those questions in order to feel comfortable making a decision.

Honor her priorities, not yours. Think of Sofat's client, Helen, and her intent to buy a home—a decision Sofat enabled. "Every woman I've met is perfectly capable of making financial decisions about her life," Sofat says. For her, it's a matter of probing the client's innate needs and preferences and giving advice accordingly.

UNDERSTAND HER

Get at the underlying emotions. Allaudin, for example, has an uncanny ability to "unravel" clients with an emphasis on exploring a client's identity with money and their personal history with it. Women open up, she says, when you invite them to talk about how they feel about money—their fears, concerns, and aspirations. Creating an emotional connection is a huge differentiator.

Go beyond the numbers. "Returns matter," says one female focus group participant. "But I can read the numbers myself. What I really want my advisor to tell me is: How will this product impact my day-to-day and the next few years?"

Ask open-ended questions. By asking about her family, an advisor can better relate a client's financial situation to her personal experiences and emotions. Huvane, for example, used to ask female clients a lot of closed questions about age, value of assets, children's names— but quickly saw eyes glaze. "So I changed it up," he says. Now, he gets the basics and then goes right to broader questions. He asks, "Tell me, when you look at your life, what's most important?" Then he starts listening. "I don't have to say another word for fifteen minutes," he says.

Read the client's body language. When Chris Dodd of Fidelity met recently with an executive whose husband had passed away, he started the discussion with a no-nonsense approach, focusing on some investment decisions. But from his experience in the military as an intelligence officer, Dodd was able to see that the woman was affronted. "Right away, I saw physical stress in her eyes and realized I wasn't being sensitive to her frame of mind," Dodd says. He shifted the conversation to focus on how she could best use life insurance proceeds to help rebalance work and life for herself and her young children.

Focus on outcomes. Design solutions that will generate returns for a real estate or retirement goal. "Somebody who asks me questions, understands my answers, and then comes back armed with solutions that genuinely address my goals, is somebody I know I can trust," a female investor told us in a focus group.

EDUCATE HER

Establish a baseline. Do not assume low confidence means low literacy. Ask questions to get a sense of her actual financial knowledge. Try questions like, "Tell me a little bit about your familiarity with this topic. What do you know already?" Start with basic concepts, but purposefully include an advanced financial term here and there in your conversations. Then take the time to get feedback so that you understand what she may have missed. This technique can go a long way to forging trust. "My advisor casually asked me personal questions and threw in a little industry jargon to gauge my reaction," says one female investor. "She caught a gap, but really boosted my confidence when she told me I am actually far more financially literate than I initially thought."

Use visuals. Bring concepts to life by creating frameworks and graphics that break down a complex idea. A male advisor at a large investment firm regularly brought the firm's chief investment officer, a whiz at creating visuals on the back of an envelope, to client meetings. Not only did he demonstrate an impressive alliance with the CIO, his clients grasped difficult concepts far more quickly.

Offer educational resources. Our data shows that advisors can boost women's confidence and feed their hunger for knowledge by creating and connecting them to online educational opportunities. Packaging product information in a way that women can bring it home and research it more deeply can also go a long way to giving women the acumen they need to make financial decisions with confidence.

ALIGN HER LIFE AND FINANCIAL GOALS

Help amplify her agency. One of the more rewarding moments in Nadia Allaudin's career was in attending a gala hosted by the city's philharmonic in honor of its benefactors—including Allaudin's clients, a married couple whose significant stock gift helped the philharmonic survive in a climate hostile to arts organizations. After an evening of incredible music, sumptuous food and wine, and memorable conversation, Allaudin turned to the wife. "I can't help thinking of the life cycle of money," Allaudin observed. "You went out and earned it, then you entrusted us to invest it, and after a year and a day you used one of your appreciated stocks to gift to charity, making it possible for this orchestra to play."

Beaming with pleasure, her client replied, "Well, it was all because of Nike!"

Reflecting on her client's comment, Allaudin says, reminds her why she spends the time she does getting to know her clients to understand their values, their goals, and what gives them a sense of meaning and purpose. "It was such a meaningful, tangible decision for her," Allaudin explains. "She remembered the exact stock that had made it possible for her and her husband to make such an impactful gift." She adds, "It reminds me that it's not just financial return that's driving them as investors."

Take a holistic approach to client satisfaction. In her work with married couples in Asia, Dominique Boer, head of relationship management for Asia and Greater China at Standard Chartered, frequently works outside the expected responsibilities of a financial advisor. For example, she assists clients who wish to obtain permanent residency in Singapore via Government Schemes (now GIS-Global Investment Scheme) and helps them look for housing and schools for their children. "It's outside of the bank's duty, but we do it to help our clients achieve their life goals," Boer says. And, she finds, when she's doing this work, women take the lead. "They want to choose where to live, which house, and which school for their children. The husband, to be perfectly honest, will typically just agree with what the wife has chosen, particularly on the life goals," she says.

Keep pace with evolving goals. While men and women both may change their decisions based on new information, women more acutely feel ignored or misunderstood if their advisor fails to keep track of their evolving needs. As Shelley O'Connor, head of field management for Morgan Stanley wealth management notes, "Women want their advisor to include them in the investing process and to make it clear how their investments align with their interests and life goals." Check-ins can be brief, but they should be frequent enough that your outreach appears to be motivated by genuine interest rather than quarterly progress reports.

Offer opportunities for her investments to reflect her values. Recognizing the demand for investments that reflect personal values, Pell's firm has developed a subspecialty in environmental, social, and governance (ESG) investing, proactively bringing ESG (also known as impact) investment options to clients. "The interest level for ESG investments among women is particularly strong, and the uptake is high."

Pell continues, "I spoke to a client I'll call Miriam about community development notes which are bundles of low-interest loans for community development projects. Miriam had a large amount of liquid cash, and she loved the idea of earning a CD-like return while funding development in local communities."

BE EFFICIENT

Manage details, streamline processes. Women favor service providers who save them time and spare them red tape. A female executive in India shared, "Frankly, I keep my account with a local bank instead of switching to a bigger one because the branch manager handles my account, and I know I will get good service without jumping through extra hoops."

Fairport Asset Management Advisor Ken Coleman notes, "When we have a female client who's an executive, one of her biggest challenges is time." Instead of going through a traditional onboarding procedure he notes, "We start by just asking for last year's tax return." This practice allows Coleman and his team to save new clients the trouble of filling out exhaustive financial background forms.

Be sensitive to time constraints. Stay aware of limits on female clients' time, particularly if they are busy professionals. "I rarely hold in-person check-ins with clients who are time-strapped," one advisor shared. "We can more reliably connect over the phone, saving her the time of traveling to my office."

Do your homework. Research her background before your meeting, to develop a good idea of who she is— both financially and personally. That way, you can skip over questions that can be easily found via LinkedIn or other public profiles and, once you've confirmed that information, you can move on to more substantive questions about her priorities and goals.

Tackle her objectives right away. Ask her to put her needs on the table from the get-go. Try a pre-meeting call or email requesting that she share three top financial objectives, which can guide your first in-person conversation. "I always emphasize, 'You are the CEO— this is *your* money. I'm the CFO, and I'm here to make you feel successful,'" a female advisor told us. "Then I ask, 'what is the most important thing that you'd like to accomplish in our time together?'"

SIX WAYS TO WIN WITH WOMEN

COMMUNICATE WELL

- ☐ *Brand yourself as a communicator*—signal a genuine desire to connect by engaging in "getting to know you" conversation.

- ☐ *Be authentic*—diverge from the script and be guided by your own views and life experience.

- ☐ *Listen actively*—demonstrate you have heard the client by repeating back what she has said and asking follow up questions.

- ☐ *Be patient*—give your client time to digest and respond, invoking the 3:1 rule.

- ☐ *Communicate on her terms*—be flexible in the mode and the frequency of communication.

CREATE A SAFE SPACE

- ☐ *Signal respect*—acknowledge her as a key decision maker at the outset of a meeting.

- ☐ *Be vulnerable*—establish meaningful dialog by opening up personally and sharing stories.

- ☐ *Make your office feel like a refuge*—create a calming environment that makes clients feel comfortable not intimidated.

- ☐ *Save the jargon, use clear language*—avoid technical financial terms and explain concepts fully but in a digestible manner.

- ☐ *Elicit questions*—take the time to encourage clients to ask questions.

- ☐ *Honor her priorities*—solve first for the client's top priorities and preferences.

UNDERSTAND HER

- ☐ *Get at the underlying emotions*—understand how she identifies with money to create an emotional connection.

- ☐ *Go beyond the numbers*—learn her personal priorities and concerns and package advice accordingly.

- ☐ *Ask open-ended questions*—start with the basics, and expand into thought-provoking questions that elicit full responses.

- ☐ *Use emotional intelligence*—read her body language and be nimble in shifting the conversation.

- ☐ *Focus on outcomes*—relate investment decisions to broader life goals.

EDUCATE HER

- ☐ *Establish a baseline*—avoid assumptions and ask questions to get a sense of her level of financial acumen.

- ☐ *Use visuals*—bring concepts to life through graphics and illustrations.

- ☐ *Offer additional resources*—connect her to online educational opportunities.

ALIGN HER LIFE AND FINANCIAL GOALS

☐ *Help amplify her agency*—understand what drives her and help her derive meaning and purpose from her financial decisions.

☐ *Take a holistic approach*—offer advice and service beyond financial products and planning.

☐ *Keep pace with evolving goals*—stay in touch with her evolving life goals and investment needs and tailor advice to match.

☐ *Offer opportunities for social investing*—offer products that address her values agenda.

BE EFFICIENT

☐ *Manage details, streamline processes*—save her time by handling paperwork and limiting unnecessary processes.

☐ *Be sensitive to time constraints*—stay aware of limits on female clients' time.

☐ *Do your homework*—research her background and develop a sense of her financial and personal life before you meet.

☐ *Tackle her objectives right away*—invite her to share her priorities; ask in advance through a pre-meeting call or email.

9

Winning Women's Business: A Road Map for Wealth Management Firms

At a recent event hosted by UBS Wealth Management in London, a pioneer female entrepreneur proved a top draw among other successful women entrepreneurs, who listened rapt as she related the story of her journey from whiz kid to business leader to donor extraordinaire. For her audience of fellow entrepreneurs and would-be philanthropists, it was a rare opportunity to hear from one of their own, network with each other, and learn how to harness their own wealth to fulfill similarly altruistic agendas.

And for UBS, it was a golden opportunity to solidify its niche among female entrepreneurs, a market segment it has quietly ring-fenced since 2006. "It's a growth market for us," observes Jamie Broderick, head of UBS wealth management in the UK. "Women entrepreneurs, like women generally, tend to be underbanked—partially because they're under-noticed and partially because they're assumed to be somewhat more risk-averse."

What differentiates UBS's approach is not so much the events it offers this group but rather, the engagement style its advisors adopt and the diversity of wealth managers that Broderick's division can boast. "Ultimately, we reach women in the marketplace best, whether they're entrepreneurs or not, by having superior client skills," he says. "Women are underserved because wealth businesses don't do as good a job at listening to clients as they should. If you do a good job of listening to their needs, and taking pains to understand the personal and emotional component of their wealth agenda, that's just good management—and in my experience female clients respond positively to this approach. If they don't feel advisors pay attention to their level of technical knowledge or their level of comfort with risk, then they feel they're just being barreled over with broadcast sales pitches."

Hence the first step to engage women, according to Broderick, is to do a better job of training client advisors to be empathetic listeners. But sustained success with this growth market, he stresses, requires more systemic changes in the firm's culture: specifically, greater diversity throughout the workforce. "You don't need to pair women client advisors with women clients or LGBT advisors with LGBT clients," he explains. "Rather, if you have a mix of ages, sexual preference, communication styles, then everyone's already sensitized to difference, and can better respond to and engage the diversity we encounter in the marketplace."

That's the starting point: a diverse population. Yet Broderick insists that firms don't go far enough to ensure that leaders, and not just advisors, embody and embrace difference. It's a matter of making them aware of the biases they harbor and apply, something best accomplished, he feels, through unconscious bias training conducted as a group. "People are perfectly willing to have their eyes opened to these things, and once they do you can have some spectacular outcomes," he says. Senior managers can manage more effectively: "they can call on people, or prompt people who are quiet, or manage the interruptions more proactively," he explains. "They can also manage the temperature in the room, so that people who aren't as assertive or who are intimidated by volatile conversations get a chance to contribute."

In his own teams, he's been that manager—the result, he says, of his own awakening as a parent to the power of proactive listening. "Slow down, pay attention, listen to other people and read their emotions," he observes, "and they will open up and talk to you and hear and listen to you better, because you are validating them." He adds, "That's what good leadership is all about, not just effective client engagement."

A NEW MODEL FOR TALENT, A NEW MARKET FOR THE INDUSTRY

Broderick and the model he's built for UBS underscore the win-win for firms of harnessing diverse talent and cultivating gender smarts—on the front lines, but also in leadership—to capture underserved market segments. Rather than rolling out another marketing campaign, the industry would be well served to diversify its workforce to better represent its high-growth target markets; to train its leaders to make sure the quietest voice in the room gets heard; and to train advisors on the front lines how to engage with women. Only by creating the kind of speak-up culture that Broderick describes can those with insight into the burgeoning female market get the airtime to share their ideas, and the backing they need to develop those ideas and pilot them in the marketplace. To unlock market-attuned innovation, senior management needs, in effect, to behave inclusively—as our 2013 research, *Innovation, Diversity and Market Growth,* so powerfully substantiates.

Inclusive leadership sets in motion a virtuous cycle that benefits both the industry and female investors. Men like Broderick who've acquired gender smarts attract female talent to financial services; more women in the business means more wealth managers who understand what women want; and women-savvy managers and advisors in turn innovate the business model to shift from product-centered to client-centered. That's a model that engages men as part of the solution and plays to women's strengths, making them more successful in the business. Our research in fact shows that advisors with gender smarts—female advisors, but also men like Huvane, who understand how women's insight, perspective and experience differs from men's—are more likely to exhibit the six behaviors we shared in Chapter 8 that are proven to win women's trust, loyalty, and satisfaction. For example, among our global cohort, female respondents who identify their advisor as having gender smarts were 30% more likely to say their advisor educates them and 27% more likely to say their advisor understands them and helps them align their investments and their life goals.

Figure 9.1
Investors whose advisor...

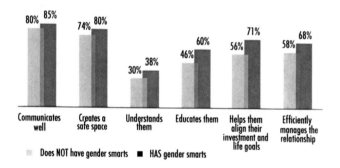

Communicates well — Does NOT have gender smarts: 80%, HAS gender smarts: 85%
Creates a safe space — 74%, 80%
Understands them — 30%, 38%
Educates them — 46%, 60%
Helps them align their investment and life goals — 56%, 71%
Efficiently manages the relationship — 58%, 68%

Does NOT have gender smarts   ■ HAS gender smarts

We see this alignment of gender smarts in Asia: women are relationship managers and investment advisors at the same rate as men, suggesting the industry is poised to capitalize on the vast and growing purse that Asian women represent.

Dominique Boer, head of relationship management for Asia and Greater China at Standard Chartered, and whose team is over 50% female, speaks to the value of that gender ratio. "Atypical of Asian culture, my female bankers don't take no for an answer. They challenge me, and that behavior helps them be the best of the best. Their confidence pays off with clients too: They encourage them to ask questions, and they do, which improves our clients' confidence in decision making. My female bankers are more willing to show vulnerability, which also engenders trust. In return, they're consistent and straightforward at communicating—the good, the bad, and the ugly. That's a recipe for developing a good client relationship and serving as a role model for their male peers."

But the virtuous cycle doesn't yet characterize financial services firms in the West. Until very recently, with the appointment of Abigail Johnson as CEO of Fidelity in 2014 and Cathy Engelbert as CEO of Deloitte in February 2015, there were no female CEOs heading up Fortune 500 financial services firms.[50] Women make up only 15.9% of these firms' executive officers.[51] This isn't for lack of ambition, CTI finds: 91% of female advisors are "very ambitious," and 75% aspire to grow their business. While women do increasingly command the middle rungs, representing 53.4% of financial managers, 40.5% of financial analysts, and 35.5% of personal financial advisors,[52] there they languish. They're absent the sponsorship that might pull them out of the marzipan layer; they're absent the feedback on executive presence that might help them attract sponsors; and, given the entrepreneurial nature of wealth advisory, they're often just invisible to leaders who might invest in their development.

Hence both at the top and on the front lines, financial services companies in the West are short on diversity. There is a need for more women in the business, but so too is there a need for more inclusive leaders like Jamie Broderick and gender-savvy advisors like Tom Huvane.

Transformation will require action on three fronts. Firms must address both the homogeneity and unconscious bias at the top to create an inclusive culture, one which foments contribution from minority voices. Once senior leaders adopt inclusive behaviors, so too will middle managers and advisors on the frontlines. To ensure leadership embodies as well as embraces difference, firms must also help women build successful careers in the business. And finally, firms must offer a differentiated client experience for women based on their unique value proposition as investors.

BUILD AN INCLUSIVE CULTURE

Engender trust through vulnerability and transparency. Conscious that wealth transfers in Asia to daughters and self-made female professionals represent her biggest opportunity, Dominique Boer recently flew 40 prospective clients from China—35 female and 5 male multimillionaires and entrepreneurs—to Singapore for a meet-and-greet. They were all friends and relatives of a female client who had relocated with her husband from Chengdu to Singapore with the help of Standard Chartered. "This lady wanted to help her friends and family do the same thing," Boer explains. "So we encouraged these women to ask us anything—to be tough on us. And they were. They asked some very direct questions about our strategy and performance. And we answered them honestly, because if you lie or embellish the truth to any client, you're finished in one second. When they asked why we had taken certain decisions about our business, I said, 'We need to realign our priorities. In your business, you'd do the same thing. We're realigning areas that are performing less well than others or are not core to our business strategy, and we're using the savings to reinvest in other parts of the bank.' Our honesty held us in good stead. Every person in that room opened an account that day. Never in my wildest dreams could I have imagined that forty multimillionaires would sign up in a single day. But I can also tell you that if I tried to sell them a product where we couldn't deliver, forty people would've walked out of the bank and taken their accounts with them."

Conduct a diagnostic—what gets measured gets addressed. Just how inclusive is your culture? Diagnostics we've performed on companies reveal a persistent disconnect between what leaders believe and what subordinates report. We've uncovered similar misperceptions among advisors on the frontlines who think they have an inclusive approach in communicating with clients and building trust but aren't meeting clients' expectations—a disconnect our dataset speaks to, as the majority of female investors in the six countries we surveyed report they do not feel understood by their advisor.

Tackle unconscious bias. "I'll see a male or even a female advisor talking to a married couple, and all of the body language is focused on the male client," says Shona Baijal, a senior client advisor and now desk head in the UBS Wealth Management division in the UK. She is working on an internal training module to help sensitize all 150 client advisors to unconscious bias, so that they can ward against it in interactions with clients. The firm hosted an academic discussion of the topic with a leading professor a few years ago to discuss unconscious bias among colleagues, but Baijal sees more potential for impact in a practical, hands-on approach. "I'm hoping we see a knock-on effect internally," she says. "We want to eliminate bias across the board."

Create role models. Because people learn by watching others and reflecting on their own personal experiences, it's critical that senior managers whose consciousness has been raised—who have the gender smarts to behave inclusively—get called out as examples of model leadership. Role models can help ignite a groundswell of "believers" eager to cascade their own epiphany.

Codifying, socializing, and rewarding inclusive behaviors catalyzes wider adoption. Bank of America is one such company working to showcase role models who clearly demonstrate inclusion. Through this work, the bank is unpacking the behaviors of inclusive leaders and disseminating their insights in bite-size learning tools (video vignettes, assessments) with the intention of initiating a shift towards greater inclusion, and building an expectation that behaviors will be discussed, embraced, and demonstrated firm-wide.

Build gender smarts on the frontlines. Fidelity recently launched an inclusive curriculum which has been embedded into training programs for its financial representatives across multiple regions in the US. The curriculum shares a compelling business case for more directly engaging women, with rich insights on the different perspectives and decision-making factors of female investors.

"We know that women are eager to learn and become more engaged in their finances, but far too many hold back from getting more involved," said Kristen Robinson, senior vice president of Women and Young Investors at Fidelity Investments. "One of the main barriers holding women back is a lack of confidence that they have the knowledge and experience to make smart choices when it comes to financial matters. This curriculum was developed to ensure that our representatives provide the best client experience possible, building women's financial confidence and making managing money and investing more accessible."

The curriculum allows various channels to reach all client-facing associates in branches and call centers, providing specialized training by role. Each module focuses on best practices in sharing information, earning trust and driving engagement among female clients, providing insights on what approaches can be effective in leading interactive discussion and collaboration, building confidence, and motivating action. Case studies and guidelines make clear how to tailor one's style to serve different client segments.

DEVELOP WINNING WOMEN

Invest in women. We've seen a number of financial services firms invest in developing female talent—from Morgan Stanley's redesign of their onboarding program for new advisors, to Goldman Sach's investment in sponsorship for their top female advisors newer to the business. Charles Schwab recognizes the benefits of a diverse and inclusive culture and launched the RIA Talent Advantage™ program to cultivate women in the registered investment advisor industry and to support them as they rise to leadership and client-facing positions.

Rethink onboarding tactics. Recognizing that female wealth advisors might be interested in a more collaborative introduction to financial advisory services work, Morgan Stanley developed its Wealth Advisory Associates (WAA) program in 2012. Piloting the initiative with a group of five associates, Scott Drever, head of financial advisor associate training at Morgan Stanley, has now expanded the program to include 300 fledgling advisors. Instead of expecting associates to start to build their own client practice after a five-month training and certification process, WAA places its associates in a complex branch role to work with established wealth advisors for a period of 12 months so that they can build networks in the firm and provide planning analysis and support to learn the Morgan Stanley planning platform before continuing in the 36-month Financial Advisor Associate program. "The program has grown because there is a lot of interest in the field," says Drever. "We get positive feedback from people in the program because of the rapport, exposure, and skills they get working alongside veteran advisors." The WAA program attracts a more diverse talent pool— roughly twice the number of women as compared to the traditional financial advisor track. The analytical support that WAA provides makes the program a win-win for firm and trainees. Morgan Stanley has already recognized its value add, with CEO James Gorman voicing his support. Drever is piloting similar programs in other client-facing positions. "Having women in client-facing roles can attract female customers, as well as provide more diverse perspectives to their Morgan Stanley colleagues."

Build pathways to sponsorship. Goldman Sachs consciously sows the seeds of sponsorship for its female
employees. The night before each stop on Goldman
Sachs' annual private wealth advisor road show last
year, the business' senior leadership, most successful
female wealth advisors, and female advisors newer to
the business got together to compare notes about how
they dealt with points of inflection in their careers. Not
only did they swap stories and advice, they deepened
ties with each other, establishing a strong foundation
for sponsorship between senior women and the next
generation of advisors. "Having the recurring opportunity to speak with some of the most senior women
in the firm about their professional paths has made a
real difference in how I perceive my own career here,"
says Megan Taylor, chief operating officer of the private
wealth management business in the firm's Investment
Management Division. "You realize just how similar
your experiences are and that you are not the only person to have ever faced a specific issue. You come away
more informed about how to effectively manage your
career and with an increased sense of community and
a desire to sponsor others. We were looking to cultivate
those same outcomes among our female wealth advisor
population." Giving women occasion to network with
each other is one part of a comprehensive strategy to
foment sponsorship at Goldman Sachs. The firm has
also seeded more formal programs across geographic
and business divisions such as Women's Career Strate-

gies Initiative (WCSI), which connects more than 300 high-performing second- and third-year female associates with senior leaders. Currently in its ninth year, WCSI has had a positive effect on female retention at the firm.

Help women crack the code of executive presence. CTI research shows that women get very little feedback when it comes to cultivating their leadership presence, which can be broken down into three components: gravitas, communication, and appearance. Schwab's RIA Talent Advantage™ is designed to help firms build a culture of inclusion and more effectively attract, promote, and retain talent at their firms to be optimally positioned to thrive in an evolving and highly competitive marketplace.

A core focus for the program is developing women's curriculum for women already working in the RIA industry. As part of the launch of its RIA Talent Advantage™, Schwab hosted a series of sessions on executive presence. At Schwab's IMPACT 2014 conference, one of the largest gatherings of registered investment advisors in the US, the firm hosted a pre-conference leadership workshop with a focus on creating a personal roadmap for executive presence. The workshop followed a webcast to build awareness among advisors on the universal dimensions of executive presence and the important role executive presence can play in helping advisors build relationships with mentors, sponsors, and clients.

Additionally, at IMPACT Schwab published a leadership piece which outlines the case for creating a diverse workforce and building an inclusive culture. "The RIA Talent Advantage™ initiative not only promotes diversity but allows other advisors to better understand what they can do to tailor their approach toward female clients," says Mary Rosai, senior vice president and head of marketing for Schwab Advisor Services.

WIN WITH WOMEN IN THE MARKET

Build awareness among firm leaders and advisors on the shifting composition of the market. The industry must recognize that women represent a significant market opportunity and move beyond one-off marketing initiatives and "women's events" to design a more integrated strategy. Firms need to build a much deeper appreciation among advisors and firm leaders on the shifting composition of the market, one that is increasingly comprised of wealth creators and decision makers. In some cases, this will require a commitment to weed out stale assumptions and deeply rooted biases that often result in a monolithic approach to the market.

Recognize how women's goals and decision-making factors vary by geography, generation, and wealth level. Winning women as clients will depend, too, on understanding how their goals and decision-making factors vary by geography, generation, and wealth level. Firms (and advisors) should be more deliberate in understanding the unique value proposition of the female segment of the market they are focused on serving. This will allow for a higher return on investment when it comes to seeding differentiated offerings for high-valued female client segments. As we saw in Chapter 3, female investors are seeking a greater basket of goods. When it comes to their service experience, banks can win women's business by equipping advisors with tools that enable them to better understand their client's unique perspective and offer a more holistic approach to financial planning and portfolio construction.

Tap the rich insights and innovative ideas of female talent in the firm. Companies that harness the innovative potential of their female talent—whose leaders are likely to value the ideas that women bring to marketing, product development, and service offerings—are likeliest to win in the marketplace, as CTI's groundbreaking research on innovation, diversity, and market growth affirms. According to 56% of our sample, leaders fail to see value in ideas they personally don't relate to or understand, which means that at companies helmed by men, women are less likely than their male colleagues to have their ideas endorsed and implemented. Firms can avert this bottleneck by hosting forums to elicit ideas from women. Companies can also reposition employee resource groups (ERGs) as business resource groups (BRGs), recalibrating affinity-group charters to focus their insight on transforming the business.

Under the sponsorship of inclusive leaders who know how to leverage women's real-world insights, BRGs can spearhead gender-smart initiatives to win women as investors.

Tailor approaches to the market by segment. Firms like US Trust have launched tailored engagement strategies to reach female high-net-worth clients. Seeing the growing market that high-net-worth women represent, the firm developed a broad initiative to address the significant and specific planning needs of women and their families. Judy Slotkin manages the effort for the New York Metro area, but the initiative is a national one. As part of the *US Trust 2013 Insights on Wealth and Worth* study, US Trust surveyed 260 high-net-worth women. "From this survey we realized high-net-worth women tend not to have comprehensive estate plans in place," Slotkin said. To increase awareness about the need for financial planning and available resources, Slotkin and her colleagues in New York designed and produced a series of four events over the last year that touched 150 high-net-worth women in the New York Metro area. The kickoff event, "Know Your Value(s)," featured *Ms.* magazine founder Gloria Steinem and Mika Brzezinski, author and co-host of *Morning Joe*.

Slotkin and her team were pleased with the results. "Our objective was to make women aware of their need to plan, give them a roadmap to follow, and demonstrate our expertise. The way we did this was to showcase our female leaders and establish a simpatico with our audience. By having female leaders be vocal on issues related to high-net-worth women, we are demonstrating our commitment to this very important audience and paving the way for our advisors to do what they do best."

Leverage new assessment tools. Firms are embracing new opportunities and creating new tools to understand the female market. In 2007, Barclays bank developed the Financial Personality Assessment to predict the investment behaviors and preferences of individual investors. The assessment asks questions to understand a client's tolerance to risk, composure in crisis, self-perception of financial expertise, and desire to delegate decision making to an advisor, among other dimensions. "With men and women, it's easy to make assumptions through a gendered lens about what the client may want. With the assessment, you have a better idea of the needs of your particular client," says Emily Haisley, a member of Barclays Behavioral Finance team. "It takes away the guesswork."

Barclays is developing new assessments, exploring questions that evaluate discipline in financial planning (i.e. financial discipline). The bank is also developing new tools, like a goal-oriented investment planner built to help users ensure they can fund future expenditures. "Often when you try to tailor things to be more appropriate for women, you build different tools or go in new directions that are better for everyone," Haisley says.

Close the confidence gap. UBS Private Wealth Management is one of several firms that have recognized the important role financial services firms can play in helping to close the confidence gap for female investors.

The annual UBS Women's Symposium was designed and launched in response to the growing awareness that most traditional wealth management initiatives fail to address the specific planning needs of women. The two-day annual event aims to educate women of all ages to empower them to take control of decisions that affect their lives and wealth. In 2014, the symposium in New York City included sessions on philanthropy, investing in women and girls, and the evolution of female empowerment. Attendees had ample time to focus on the community-building aspects, as well, says Judy Spalthoff, executive director and head of WMA Business Development. Spalthoff, the creator of the Women's Symposium, views the event as the first milestone achievement in the firm's long-term strategic goal to deepen relationships with female clients, and prospects and their families. UBS is exploring the idea of hosting regional events, as well as developing a scalable financial literacy program that advisors can deliver to their clients either in person or digitally.

Invest in values. With the emergence of demand from clients, more financial services firms are launching investment products that allow clients to align their values with their investing dollars. Firms like Morgan Stanley have developed an impacting investment platform, while a handful of investment firms such as Pax Ellevate Asset Management and US Trust have recently launched products that enable clients to invest in diversity.

Like Geri Eisenman Pell at Pell Wealth Management, Morgan Stanley has found that its individual and institutional clients increasingly want to invest their assets in ways consistent with their values and beliefs. To meet this need, Morgan Stanley created a robust investment framework called "Investing with Impact," launched in April 2012. This flexible framework allows clients to work with advisors to build a portfolio that screens out companies with practices inconsistent with the investor's values, and to actively seek like-minded companies. Instead of focusing solely on environmental impact, the fund allows clients to prioritize different environmental, social, or governance (ESG) issues of interest. All of these ESG investment vehicles have been evaluated for financial integrity and return potential, as well as social impact, making Investing with Impact an exceptionally well-tailored product to meet the needs of socially minded female investors.

In 2014, Pax World Management LLC and Ellevate Asset Management LLC partnered to launch the Pax Ellevate Global Women's Index Fund. The Fund is the first and only mutual fund in the United States that focuses on investing in companies that are global leaders in advancing women. Among the companies in the Fund, 32% of board seats and 25% of executive management positions are held by women, as compared to global averages of 12% and 11% respectively. According to Ellevate Asset Management LLC Fund Principal Sallie Krawcheck, "research indicates that companies with more women in senior management have higher returns on capital, lower volatility, greater client focus, increased innovation, and greater long-term orientation." And as a result, says Krawcheck, "they should also deliver better stockholder returns over time."

US Trust also recognized the growing demand by clients for opportunities to invest in women. Started in 2012 as a collaboration between US Trust (the private wealth management arm of Bank of America) and the Women's Foundation of California (a nonprofit organization dedicated to supporting women's economic security), the Women and Girls Equality Strategy has evolved into one of the few investing strategies to focus solely on backing companies that promote gender equality throughout their entire corporation. The strategy invests in companies that excel according to a specific set of criteria that reflect proprietary research on labor practices, pay equality, and access to capital and jobs for women. In addition, companies are evaluated on their recruitment, training, and advancement of women, as well as their focus on materially benefiting the lives of women and girls globally.

Long-term, US Trust wants to demonstrate that the application of a gender lens in portfolios is value-enhancing. "Ten years from now, we believe it will be adopted into the mainstream investment process, as you can already see the impact of a gender lens on issues such as the power of women consumers in emerging markets, or the risk of investing in a drug company that has not tested drugs equally on men and women," says Jackie VanderBrug, a US Trust senior vice president and investment strategist.

THREE WAYS FOR FIRMS TO WIN WITH WOMEN

BUILD AN INCLUSIVE CULTURE

- ☐ *Engender trust through vulnerability and transparency*—create an honest dialogue with clients to establish credibility and trust

- ☐ *Conduct a diagnostic*—create a baseline set of measurements to develop a clear understanding of where your firm stands.

- ☐ *Tackle unconscious bias*—develop internal training modules to ward against bias in advisor-client interactions.

- ☐ *Create role models*—call out senior managers with gender smarts as examples of model leadership.

- ☐ *Build gender smarts on the frontlines*—develop an inclusive advisor curriculum that demonstrates the business case for targeting women investors.

DEVELOP WINNING WOMEN

- ☐ *Invest in women*—raise women up to leadership positions, and bring in more women at all firm levels.

- ☐ *Rethink onboarding tactics*—consider collaborative, group-based introductions to financial advisory work.

- ☐ *Build pathways to sponsorship*—cultivate sponsorship of top female talent.

- ☐ *Help women crack the code of executive presence*—develop programs that help women acquire and exude gravitas, communicate effectively, and appear both professional and authentic.

WIN WITH WOMEN IN THE MARKET

☐ *Build awareness among firm leaders and advisors on the shifting composition of the market*—design integrated strategies to move beyond traditional assumptions about women investors.

☐ *Recognize how women's goals and decision-making factors vary by geography, generation, and wealth level*—help advisors to identify and acknowledge the unique qualities of their female investors.

☐ *Tap the rich insights and innovative ideas of female talent in the firm*—create opportunities for women to share their ideas; leverage ERGs.

☐ *Tailor approaches to the market by segment*—ensure marketing and engagement strategies acknowledge and address different segments of the female market.

☐ *Leverage new assessment and reporting tools*—develop tools that allow advisors to more deeply understand investor behaviors, preferences, discipline, and goals.

☐ *Close the confidence gap*—develop enriching programs to offer financial acumen and confidence to female clients.

☐ *Invest in values*—meet women's desire to invest in companies that promote social well being and diversity.

APPENDIX

METHODOLOGY

The research consists of a survey, Insights in-Depth® sessions (a proprietary web-based tool used to conduct voice-facilitated virtual focus groups) involving more than 100 people from our Task Force organizations, and more than 60 one-on-one interviews.

The survey, conducted online in November 2013 through February 2014, sampled 5,924 respondents (4,200 men and 1,724 women: 1,101 US, 1,000 UK, 1,008 China, 1,007 India, 808 Singapore, and 1,000 Hong Kong), aged 21 and older. In addition, screening was done to confirm personal income of $100,000 or more, or investable assets of at least $500,000. Data in the US were weighted to be representative of the US population on key demographics (age, sex, race/ethnicity, region, education, and income). The base used for statistical testing was the effective base. Data for the UK, China, India, Singapore, and Hong Kong were not weighted.

The survey was conducted by Knowledge Networks under the auspices of the Center for Talent Innovation, a nonprofit research organization. Knowledge Networks was responsible for the data collection, while the Center for Talent Innovation conducted the analysis.

In the charts, percentages may not always add up to 100 because of computer rounding or the acceptance of multiple responses to questions.

CHARTS

This appendix includes many data points from our research on female investors across US, UK, India, China, Hong Kong, and Singapore. It is intended to provide a broader context for comparisons and the analysis of country-specific themes as well as richer data on sub-segments of the female market for India, China, Hong Kong, and Singapore.

UNITED STATES

Figure A.1
Respondents without financial advisors
(US)

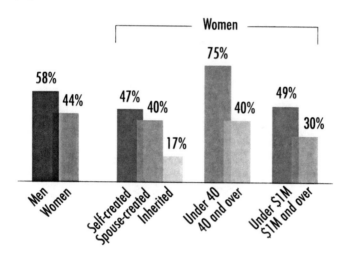

Figure A.2
Respondents who feel their advisor doesn't understand them
(US)

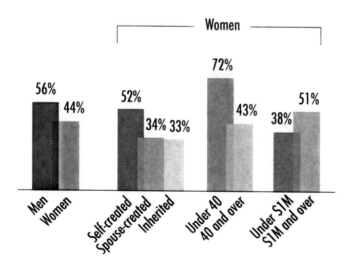

Figure A.3
Do you want to invest in any of the following causes?
(US)

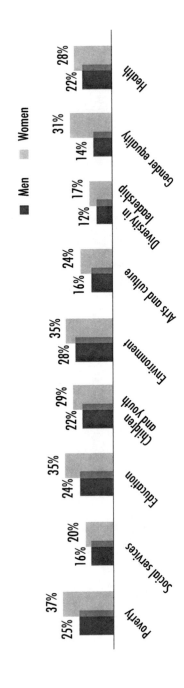

UNITED KINGDOM

Figure A.4
Respondents without financial advisors
(UK)

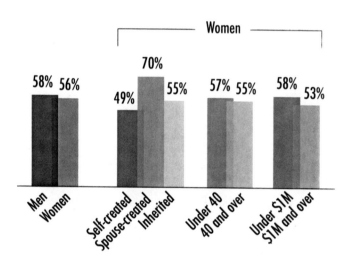

Figure A.5
Respondents who feel their advisor doesn't understand them
(UK)

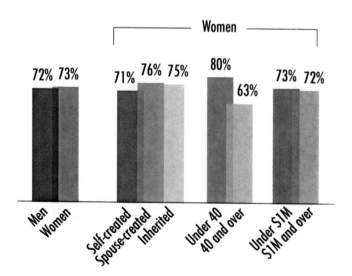

INDIA

Figure A.6
Respondents without financial advisors
(India)

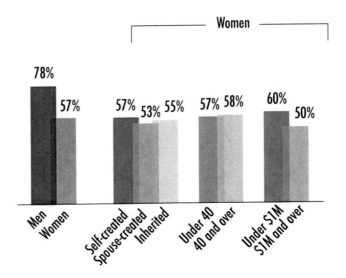

Figure A.7
Respondents who feel their advisor doesn't understand them
(India)

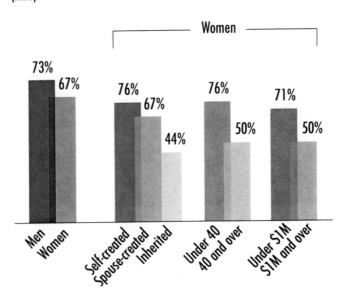

Figure A.8
Perceived vs. actual risk appetite †
(India)

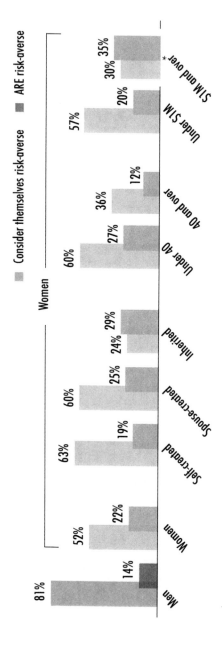

■ Consider themselves risk-averse   ■ ARE risk-averse

Women

	Consider themselves risk-averse	ARE risk-averse
Men	81%	14%
Women	52%	22%
Self-treated	63%	19%
Spouse-created	60%	25%
Inherited	24%	29%
Under 40	60%	27%
40 and over	36%	12%
Under $1M	57%	20%
$1M and over *	30%	35%

* Sample size under 25

Figure A.9
Do you want to invest in/donate to any of the following causes?
(Indian women)

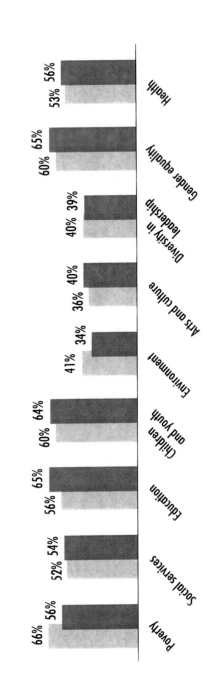

■ Want to invest in   ■ Want to donate to

CHINA

Figure A.10
Respondents without financial advisors
(China)

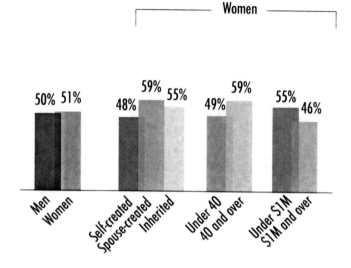

Figure A.11
Respondents who feel their advisor doesn't understand them
(China)

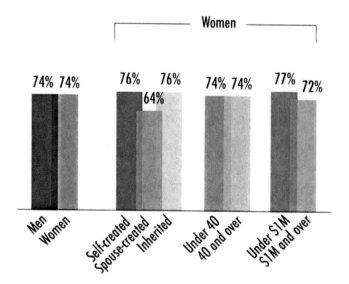

Figure A.12
Perceived vs. actual risk appetite
(China)

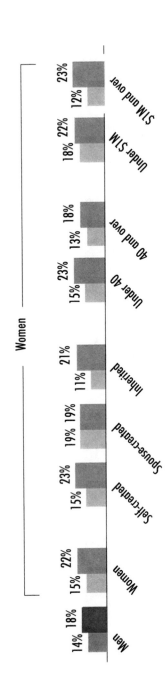

Figure A.13
Do you want to invest in/donate to any of the following causes?
(Chinese women)

■ Want to invest in   ■ Want to donate to

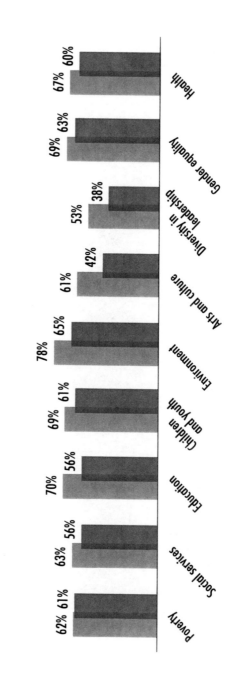

Cause	Want to invest in	Want to donate to
Poverty	62%	61%
Social services	63%	56%
Education	70%	56%
Children and youth	69%	61%
Environment	78%	65%
Arts and culture	61%	42%
Diversity in leadership	53%	38%
Gender equality	69%	63%
Health	67%	60%

HONG KONG

Figure A.14
Respondents without financial advisors
(HK)

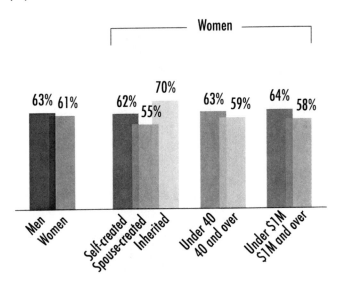

Figure A.15
Respondents who feel their advisor doesn't understand them
(HK)

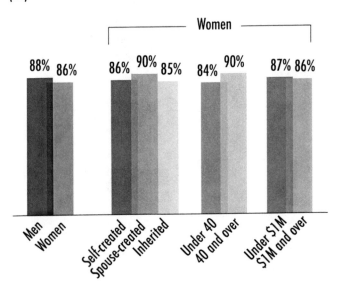

Figure A.16
Perceived vs. actual risk appetite
(HK)

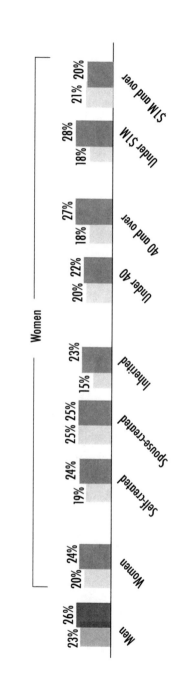

■ Consider themselves risk-averse   ■ ARE risk-averse

Women

Men: 23% 26%
Women: 20% 24%
Self-created: 19% 24%
Spouse-created: 25% 25%
Inherited: 15% 23%
Under 40: 20% 22%
40 and over: 18% 27%
Under $1M: 18% 28%
$1M and over: 21% 20%

Figure A.17
Do you want to invest in/donate to any of the following causes?
(HK women)

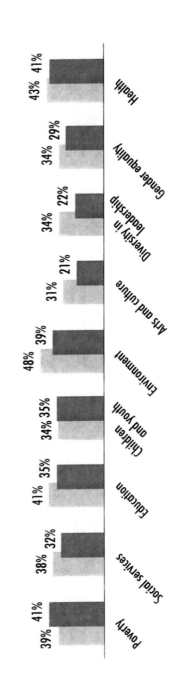

SINGAPORE

Figure A.18
Respondents without financial advisors
(SG)

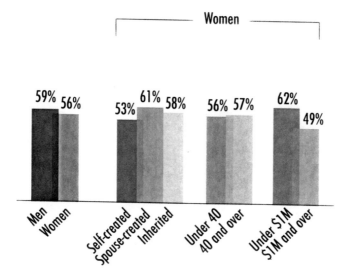

Figure A.19
Respondents who feel their advisor doesn't understand them
(SG)

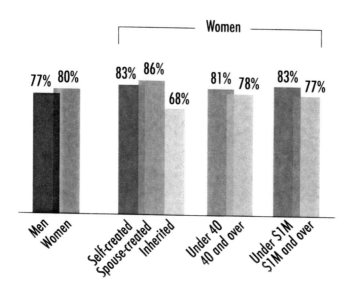

Figure A.20
Perceived vs. actual risk appetite
(SG)

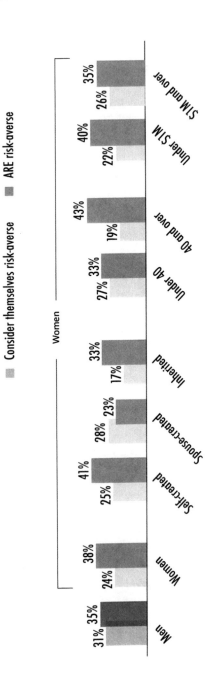

Figure A.21
Do you want to invest in/donate to any of the following causes?
(SG women)

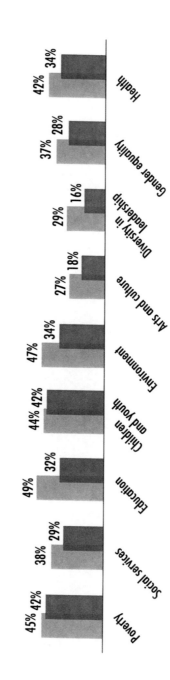

Want to invest in   ■ Want to donate to

Cause	Want to invest in	Want to donate to
Health	42%	34%
Gender equality	37%	28%
Diversity in leadership	29%	16%
Arts and culture	27%	18%
Environment	47%	34%
Children and youth	44%	42%
Education	49%	32%
Social services	38%	29%
Poverty	45%	42%

ACKNOWLEDGMENTS

In many ways this book represents an intersection of my professional and personal life. It therefore gives me particular pleasure to acknowledge the extensive support I have received from family, friends, and colleagues. My husband, in particular, has been an endless source of encouragement. His generous support, sage advice, and gender smarts have given me resilience and conviction throughout this journey. And a special thank you to my parents who humbly ensured I was afforded opportunities to flourish.

I am deeply appreciative to Sylvia Ann Hewlett whose inspiration and leadership was critical to this project. Her sponsorship and commitment seeded a vision for making this book a reality.

I owe a particular debt of gratitude to Melinda Marshall, Julia Taylor Kennedy, Melody Nixon, Catherine Fredman, Laura Sherbin, Pooja Jain-Link, Peggy Shiller, and Charlene Thrope. Without their extraordinary writing, editing, and research skills, I could not have met the ambitious deadlines of this fast-track book. I am extremely grateful.

I would like to thank our lead corporate sponsors—Michelle Gadsden-Williams (Credit Suisse); Keri Matthews, Nisha Rao, Guelabatin Sun, and Eileen Taylor (Deutsche Bank); Caroline Carr and Megan Taylor (Goldman Sachs); Susan Reid and Kara Underwood (Morgan Stanley); Jacqueline Rolf (Standard Chartered Bank); Alex Hiller, Nia Joynson-Romanzina, and Judy Spalthoff (UBS)—for their generous support which goes well beyond funding. Over this past year these corporate leaders have provided precious access and lent wise counsel. I am delighted to see their courageous efforts to drive change and am hugely grateful.

There are many academic and industry experts in our midst who lent advice and counsel. In particular, I would like to acknowledge Isobel Coleman, Mellody Hobson, Sallie Krawcheck, Helena Morrissey, and Jacki Zehner.

I am grateful to the cochairs and members of the Task Force for Talent Innovation for their belief in the importance of this study and their ongoing commitment to the work of the Center.

A special thank you to the efforts of the CTI team, specifically Liz Armstrong, Joseph Cervone, Randy Clinton, Isis Fabian, Tai Green, Kennedy Ihezie, Zachary Insani, Silvia Marte, and Jennifer Zephirin. Thanks also to the Hewlett Consulting Partners team, Noni Allwood, Carolyn Buck Luce, Terri Chung, Fabiola Dieudonné, Colin Elliott, Mark Fernandez, Wendy Hutter, Lawrence Jones, Deidra Mascoll, Ripa Rashid, Sandra Scharf, and Janice Yang for their support.

Thanks also to Nadia Allaudin, Phillip Anderson, Shona Baijal, Jason Baron, Subha Barry, Eleanor Blayney, Dominique Boer, Jamie Broderick, Melanie Cassoff, Mark Chamberlain, Kenneth Coleman, Mabel Chua, Wendy Cohen, Fiona Crozier, Nikolay Djibankov, Scott Drever, Wendi Eckardt, Eve Ellis, Courtney Emerson, Rob Farmer, Lori Feinsilver, Gail Fierstein, Roopa Foley, Tara Gonsalves, Caroline Gundeck, Judy Hsu, Tom Huvane, Deborah Jackson, Naazneen Karmali, Chanda Kochhar, Florence Kui, Carolyn Leonard, David Lessing, Marina Lui, Olivia Lum, Kathleen McQuiggan, Megan Mitchell, Rajashree Nambiar, Siri Nomme, Brian O'Connor, Shelley O'Connor, Geri Eisenman Pell, Andrea Pactor, Paula Polito, Nate Prosser, Rajan Raju, Kristen Robinson, Mary Rosai, Anu Sarkar, Judy Slotkin, Anna Sofat, Natalie Straub, Namrata Suri, Pamela Thomas-Graham, Jackie VanderBrug, Sunita Wadekar, Natasha Williams, Valerie Wong, Sheau Yuen Tan, and the women and men who took part in focus groups and Insights In-Depth® sessions.

ENDNOTES

1. Peter Damisch, Monish Kumar, Anna Zakrewski, and Natalia Zhiglinskaya, *Leveling the Playing Field: Upgrading the Wealth Management Experience for Women*, The Boston Consulting Group, July 2010, 2, http://www.bcg.com/documents/file56704.pdf.

2. Capgemini and Merrill Lynch Wealth Management, *World Wealth Report 2011*, Capgemini and Merrill Lynch Wealth Management, 2011, 24, http://www.ml.com/media/114235.pdf.

3. Goldman Sachs and Global Markets Institute, *The Power of the Purse: Gender Equality and Middle-Class Spending*, Goldman Sachs Group, August 5, 2009, 10, http://www.goldmansachs.com/our-thinking/focus-on/investing-in-women/bios-pdfs/power-of-purse.pdf.

4. Citigroup Inc., "A Glimpse into the SHE-conomy: Women are Making the Topic of Money Less Taboo," 2010, http://www.citigroup.com/citi/news/2010/100201a.htm.

5. Barclays Wealth, *Barclays Wealth Insights Volume 2: A Question of Gender*, (London: Barclays Wealth and Economist Intelligence Unit, 2007), https://wealth.barclays.com/content/dam/bwpublic/global/documents/wealth_management/insights2-gender-uk.pdf.

6. BlackRock, *U.S. Investor Pulse Survey 2013: What Investors Are Thinking*, BlackRock, August/September 2013, http://www.blackrock.com/investing/literature/press-release/global-investor-pulse-gender-findings.pdf.

7. Peter Damisch et al., *Leveling the Playing Field*, 2.

8. Stephanie Holland, "Marketing to Women Quick Facts," She-conomy.com, accessed February 19, 2015, http://she-conomy.com/report/marketing-to-women-quick-facts.

9. Sylvia Ann Hewlett and Ripa Rashid, with Catherine Fredman, Maggie Jackson, and Laura Sherbin, *The Battle for Female Talent in Emerging Markets*, (New York: Center for Work Life Policy, 2010).

10. World Bank, *World Development Report 2012: Gender Equality and Development*, (Washington, DC: The International Bank for Reconstruction and Development/World Bank, 2011), 3, https:// siteresources.worldbank.org/INTWDR2012/Resources /7778105-1299699968583/7786210-1315936222006 /Complete-Report.pdf.

11. Michael J. Silverstein and Kate Sayre "The Female Economy," *Harvard Business Review*, September 2009, https://hbr .org/2009/09/the-female-economy.

12. The World Bank, *Women's Economic Opportunities in the Formal Private Sector in Latin America and the Caribbean*, (Washington, D.C.: The World Bank, 2010), 126.

13. Center for Women's Business Research, *The Economic Impact of Women-Owned Businesses in the United States*, Center for Women's Business Research, October 2009, 9, http://www.nwbc .gov/sites/default/files/economicimpactstu.pdf.

14. Ibid., 1.

15. Andrea Navarro, "The World's Richest Women 2014," *Forbes*, March 3, 2014, http://www.forbes.com/sites /andreanavarro/2014/03/03/the-worlds-richest-women-2014/.

16. Ruth Sealy and Susan Vinnicombe, "The Female FTSE Board Report 2014: Milestone or Millstone?" (Cranfield, UK: Cranfield University, 2014).

17. Catalyst, "Catalyst Census: Fortune 500 Appendix 8—Women's Representation by NAICS Industry," Catalyst Inc., December 10, 2013, http://www.catalyst.org/knowledge/2013-catalyst-census -fortune-500-appendix-8-womens-representation-naics-industry.

18. Currency in the UK, India, China, Hong Kong, and Singapore was converted to US dollars.

19. John J. Havens and Paul G. Schervish, *A Golden Age of Philanthropy? The Impact of the Great Wealth Transfer on Greater Boston*, Boston Foundation, May 2006, 6, http://www .bc.edu/bc_org/rvp/pubaf/06/GoldenAge.pdf.

20. Ibid, 9.

21. Luisa Kroll, "The Rarer Sex: The Self-Made Women Billionaires 2013," *Forbes*, March 6, 2013, http://www.forbes.com/sites /luisakroll/2013/03/06/the-rarer-sex-the-self-made-women -billionaires-of-2013/.

22. Susan Josephs, "Lori Ann Goldman: Transforming Spanx into a Multimillion-Dollar Business," *Jewish Woman International Magazine*, fall 2012, http://www.jwi.org/page .aspx?pid=1544#sthash.7mIYT13q.XrILUWh5.dpbs.

23. Frank Tong, "Chinese Online Retailer Dangdang Reports 22% Sales Growth in 2013," *Internet Retailer*, April 10, 2014, https:// www.internetretailer.com/2014/04/10/chinese-e-retailer -dangdang-reports-22-sales-growth-2013.

24. Stephanie Baker, "Morrissey Topples Old Boys as Money Manager with Nine Children," *Bloomberg News*, May 23, 2011, http://www.bloomberg.com/news/articles/2011-05-23 /morrissey-topples-old-boys-as-money-manager-with-nine -children.

25. Forbes, "The World's Billionaires: #5 Larry Ellison," accessed April 17, 2014, http://www.forbes.com/profile/larry-ellison/.

26. The Oscars, "86th Oscars® Nominations Announced," January 16, 2014, https://www.oscars.org/sites/default/files/86aa -nominations-announcement.pdf.

27. Tracey Longo, "The Emerging Profile of Women Investors," *Financial Advisor*, August 1, 2008, http://www.fa-mag.com /news/the-emerging-profile-of-women-investors-1961.html.

28. MileStone Bank, "Financial Empowerment for Women," February 4, 2009, http://milestonebank.blogspot.com/2009/02/financial -empowerment-for-women.html.

29. Havens and Schervish, *Golden Age of Philanthropy,* 9.

30. Data on respondents in the US from the survey CTI conducted online in 2013 that culminated in its *Harnessing the Power of the Purse: Female Investors and Global Opportunities for Growth* report.

31. James Heintz, *Globalization, Economic Policy and Employment: Poverty and Gender Implications*, (Geneva: International Labour Organization, 2006), 12-13, http://www.rrojasdatabank.info /iloheintz06.pdf.

32. Grameen Bank, "Grameen Bank Monthly Update for January 2015," February 4, 2015, 421, http://www.grameen.com/index .php?option=com_content&task=view&id=452&Itemid=84.

33. Forbes, *Next-Generation Philanthropy: Changing the World*, (New York: Forbes Insights, 2012), 20, http://www.agefiactifs .com/sites/agefiactifs.com/files/files/2013/12/4PG7JWVI _7847FCreditSuissePhilanthropyREPORT091712(2).pdf.

34. Erin Carlyle, "Liesel Pritzker Simmons Sued Her Family and Got $500 Million, but She's No Trust Fund Baby," *Forbes*, December 2, 2013, http://www.forbes.com/sites/erincarlyle/2013/11/17/liesel-pritzker-simmons-sued-her-family-and-got-500-million-but-shes-no-trust-fund-baby/.

35. Rachel Nuwer, "China Has More Self-Made, Female Billionaires than Any Other Country," Smithsonian.com, September 19, 2013, http://www.smithsonianmag.com/smart-news/china-has-more-self-made-female-billionaires-than-any-other-country-9904311/.

36. Forbes, "Olivia Lum," accessed February 16, 2015, http://www.forbes.com/profile/olivia-lum/.

37. The World Bank, "Global Economic Prospects," accessed February 16, 2015, http://www.worldbank.org/en/publication/global-economic-prospects/data?variable=NYGDPMKTPKDZ&region=EAP.

38. World Bank, "Labor Force Participation Rate, Female (% of Female Population Ages 15+) (Modeled ILO Estimate)," accessed February 16, 2015, http://data.worldbank.org/indicator/SL.TLF.CACT.FE.ZS.

39. Russell Flannery, "Inside the 2013 Forbes China 400: A Record 168 Billionaires," *Forbes*, October 10, 2013, http://www.forbes.com/sites/russellflannery/2013/10/21/inside-the-2013-forbes-china-400-a-record-168-billionaires/.

40. Nitya Rao, "Women's Access to Land: An Asian Perspective," UN Women, September 2011, http://www.un.org/womenwatch/daw/csw/csw56/egm/Rao-EP-3-EGM-RW-30Sep-2011.pdf.

41. Karl F. Inderfurth and Persis Khambatta, "India's Economy: The Other Half," U.S.-India Insight, (Washington, D.C.: Center for Strategic & International Studies, February 2012), http://csis.org/files/publication/120222_WadhwaniChair_USIndiaInsight.pdf.

42. *Global Education Digest 2010: Comparing Education Statistics across the World*, (Montreal: UNESCO Institute for Statistics, 2010), http://www.uis.unesco.org/Library/Documents/GED_2010_EN.pdf.

43. Sylvia Ann Hewlett, Ripa Rashid, and Lauren Leader-Chivee with Catherine Fredman, *The Battle for Female Talent in India*, (New York: Center for Work Life Policy, 2010).

44. Accenture, *Understanding the High Net Worth Market in China*, Accenture, 2012, 2, http://www.accenture.com/SiteCollectionDocuments/PDF/Accenture-CM-AWAMS-POV-High-Net-Worth-China-Final-Oct-2012.pdf.

45. Russell Flannery, "The Billionaire Chus and Kingston Financial Look to Make a Mark beyond Hong Kong," *Forbes*, May 4, 2012, http://www.forbes.com/sites/russellflannery/2012/05/04/the-billionaire-chus-and-kingston-financial-look-to-make-a-mark-beyond-hong-kong/.

46. Yuval Atsmon, Diane Ducarme, Max Magni, and Cathy Wu "Luxury without Borders: China's New Class of Shoppers Take on the World," McKinsey & Company, December 2012, https://solutions.mckinsey.com/insightschina/_SiteNote/WWW/GetFile.aspx?uri=%2Finsightschina%2Fdefault%2Fen-us%2Fabout%2Four_publications%2FFiles%2Fwp2055036759%2FLuxury%20Without%20Borders%20China%E2%80%99s%20New%20Class%20of%20Shoppers%20Take%20on%20the%20World_fd6a761f-2b88-4e8f-a7cc-8afac03a88f1.pdf.

47. Sanat Valikappen, "In Asia, the Wealth Management Field Favors Women," *Bloomberg Businessweek*, April 18, 2013, http://www.bloomberg.com/bw/articles/2013-04-18/in-asia-the-wealth-management-field-favors-women.

48. Data on respondents working in finance is derived from the survey CTI conducted online in 2013 that culminated in its *Innovation, Diversity and Market Growth* report. The survey sampled men and women aged 21-62 with at least a college degree working in white-collar occupations at companies with at least 50 employees.

49. Sylvia Ann Hewlett, Melinda Marshall, and Laura Sherbin, with Tara Gonzales, *Innovation, Diversity and Market Growth*, (New York: Center for Talent Innovation, 2013).

50. Michael Rapoport and Julie Steinberg, "Deloitte Taps Woman, a First, for CEO Post," *Wall Street Journal*, February 9, 2015, http://www.wsj.com/articles/deloitte-taps-cathy-engelbert-as-chief-executive-1423492486.

51. Catalyst, "Catalyst Census: Fortune 500 Appendix 8—Women's Representation by NAICS Industry."

52. Bureau of Labor Statistics, "Current Population Survey, Annual Averages Table 11: Employed Persons by Detailed Occupation, Sex, Race, and Hispanic or Latino Ethnicity," United States Department of Labor, 2014, http://www.bls.gov/cps/cpsaat11.htm.

INDEX

CPSIA information can be obtained at www.ICGtesting.com
Printed in the USA
LVOW10s2248270515

440070LV00003B/16/P